Silver Threads

Making wire filigree jewelry

Jeanne Rhodes-Moen

I wish to dedicate this book as follows:
To Bjørn, who taught me the basics of filigree.
To Linda, my first customer, who said, "If you make it, I'll buy it!"
To Randy, who taught me polishing and the meaning of quality work.
To Gillan, who helped me believe in myself, my work, and life again.
To my daughters Kaja and Thea, who put up with me during the writing process!
Also, special thanks to Ruth, Lorna, Terrie, and Ken for reading over and giving me feedback on the projects and chapters.

Garfield quote used courtesy of Jim Davis and Paws, Inc., Albany, Indiana.

Printed in the United States of America

10 9 8 7 6 1 2 3 4 5

Visit our Web site at kalmbachbooks.com
Secure online ordering available

Publisher's Cataloging-In-Publication
(Prepared by The Donohue Group, Inc.)

Rhodes-Moen, Jeanne.
   Silver threads : making wire filigree jewelry / Jeanne Rhodes-Moen.

   p.: ill. ; cm.

   ISBN-13: 978-0-87116-221-2
   ISBN-10: 0-87116-221-0

1. Jewelry making--Handbooks, manuals, etc. 2. Filigree. 3. Wire craft. 4. Silver jewelry--Handbooks, manuals, etc. I. Title.

TT212 .R46 2006
739.27

These designs are for your personal use. They are not intended for resale.

contents

I've been doing filigree since 1988 and love the technique. It was the first real silverwork I did, and I will probably be doing it for the rest of my life. My technique is based on the Norwegian form of filigree, but my style is my own.

In this book, I'll teach you to make the basic shapes and embellishments used in filigree. I have also included 12 projects, ranging from beginning to intermediate/advanced levels. These projects will teach you how to do filigree work that is similar to my personal style. This book is intended to be hands-on; I've provided clear step-by-step instructions and photography for each project.

Although I hope you enjoy the technique and learn to make all of the projects with ease, I do want to clarify one thing. I use these projects to teach a technique, but aside from the first earring project, which is a traditional Norwegian design, all the projects are my own copyrighted designs. Therefore, these projects are intended to teach you, but they are intended for personal use only. If you wish, you may make some to give as gifts. However, you are not permitted to mass-produce these projects or use them for retail or wholesale purposes.

If you have chosen this book, I'm hoping that you want to fully learn this technique, not just copy what I do. Unlock your own creativity! Filigree is open to an infinite number of designs, and I hope you experiment and develop your own style. If you make any of these projects or use these techniques to develop your own filigree designs, I would love to see them. I'm creating a section on my Web site for readers' designs; if you'd like to share yours, send photos to bookdesigns@jeannius.com.

So hop in with both feet and have fun. Don't be discouraged if some of your early attempts melt or don't look exactly like the photos in this book. You're here to learn, and I'm here to teach!

—*Jeanne Rhodes-Moen*

author's NOTE

"It's amazing what one can accomplish when one doesn't know what one can't do!!" —Garfield the Cat

The first reaction most people have when they look at metal filigree work is, "Wow! How did they do that? I could never make that. It's too complicated—too delicate." To such comments, all I can say is to keep Garfield's words of wisdom in mind when working with filigree.

When I began making silver jewelry, the first work I did was filigree, but I didn't know filigree was supposed to be difficult. The first stone I cut was an opal—a stone even experienced jewelrymakers shy away from. Some people would say that I've done things backward, that I didn't start at the "beginning." But I didn't know there was a "beginning." I only knew that I wanted to make filigree jewelry, the opportunity presented itself, and I learned.

I began my career in jewelry design quite by accident. Back in 1987, when the New Age fad came into full bloom, I was a college student who couldn't afford to spend $60 or more on a piece of crystal jewelry. But I could buy 50-cent Arkansas quartz crystals at the Smithsonian Natural History Museum in Washington, DC, and I could buy craft wire and supplies at a local craft store—so I made my own crystal jewelry! One of my college professors liked my work and asked me to make a set for her, too. I began experimenting with quartz and other crystals, bead caps, beading wire, and lots of cyanoacrylate glue.

I made and sold enough jewelry to buy myself a student ticket to Norway to visit my then-fiancé, Bjørn Moen. As it turned out, Bjørn had once wanted to make jewelry himself. (During the 1970s, Bjørn and his father had taken courses in the basic *sølje* technique, the Norwegian form of filigree work used to decorate Norway's national costumes.) But life intervened, and Bjørn set aside jewelrymaking to pursue other interests over the next decade and a half.

That summer in Norway, Bjørn dragged all the supplies out of storage and showed me the basics: how to cut, bend, and form filigree shapes and how to solder and pickle metal. I made four simple shapes—using an antiquated torch with a mouthpiece I had to blow into to mix air with the propane!

Despite working with such outmoded tools, I was hooked. When I returned home, I bought a modern torch, a bottle of muriatic acid (used for cleaning bricks, this is actually a weak

introduction

solution of hydrochloric acid), a few basic tools, and some silver wire. I began experimenting and eventually found a way to make filigree wire. I also discovered what worked and didn't work, and just how much heat I could use before my project self-destructed. I found that I could not solder with stones in place (at least not the many quartz stones I had). I also learned that while muriatic acid worked to pickle the metal, it rusted my tools and, if I didn't want holes in my clothes, I had to add baking soda to the rinse water to neutralize the acid.

Since then, I've picked up many more tips—from books, goldsmiths, and even the Internet, but I'm largely self-taught. And if I can do it, so can you. Filigree work isn't hard; the only hard part is adjusting your mindset, and this book will help you do just that. So turn the page to learn how you, too, can create beautiful filigree jewelry.

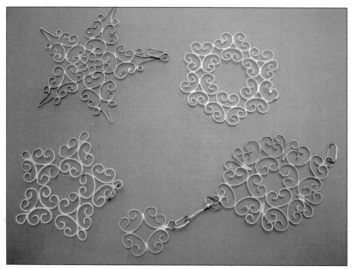

Some of my first filigree pieces. Take a close look at the shapes involved; you'll use them all in the projects that follow.

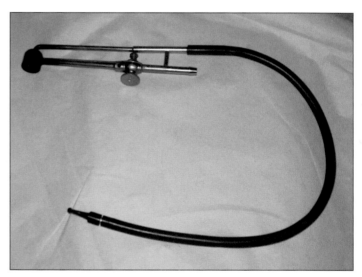

My first torch, operated by blowing air into the mouthpiece.

introduction

filigree
A BRIEF HISTORY

The origin of the word *filigree* can be traced back to 17th-century France as *filigreen* (or *filigrane*) and in Italy as *filigrana*. Both come from the Latin words *filum* (thread) and *granum* (seed). The dictionary defines filigree as:

1. Ornamental work of fine (typically gold or silver) wire formed into delicate tracery.

2. A thing resembling such fine ornamental work.

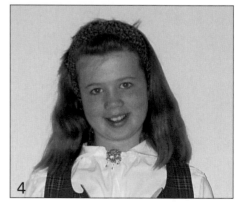

Artisans in many parts of the world, including Asia, Russia, Scandinavia, Italy, the Middle East, India, Africa, and even Mexico and South America, practice the ancient art of filigree. This metal art, however, did not develop in North America or Australia. With people from such diverse countries working in filigree, it is not surprising that the types of objects made are equally diverse. In the Orissa district in India, for example, filigree artists focus on enormous sculptures composed of thousands of individual pieces of wire. In other lands, filigree work is more often devoted to small, lightweight ornaments for body, costume, or home.

Artists traditionally use silver for their filigree work, although a few use "German silver," a variety of wire composed of less-expensive nickel. Still other artisans, primarily those in Italy and some in Africa, have transferred the technique to working with gold.

While the technique I present in this book has its roots in Norway, I strayed far from the traditional discipline and created my own style. This is what you must strive to do—learn a technique and then apply it in new ways to make it your own. You will learn my technique in this book, but as you produce more and more filigree, you'll develop your own style.

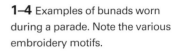

5

6

7

8

9

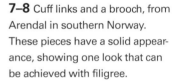

10

1–4 Examples of bunads worn during a parade. Note the various embroidery motifs.

5–6 Two traditional sølje brooches: silver from the Vest-Agder region and gold vermeil from western Norway.

7–8 Cuff links and a brooch, from Arendal in southern Norway. These pieces have a solid appearance, showing one look that can be achieved with filigree.

9 A brooch with a square center, rather than the traditional round center. Although this photo does not show the dangles fully, they are also nontraditional, and more elaborate than usual.

10 Sølje pieces from the Setesdal area. These were likely created with techniques similar to the ones you'll learn in this book.

TRADITIONAL FILIGREE

The following areas feature varying styles of filigree in the traditional sense, from small, delicate pieces of jewelry to large sculptures. Study these examples of filigree from around the world, and draw inspiration from them!

Norway

Patterns similar to filigree have been spotted in Viking jewelry as early as AD 800. Interestingly, the patterns then disappeared for several centuries. Danish goldsmiths brought them back to Norway in the late 17th and early 18th centuries, and the renowned Lorents Anderson is considered Norway's first filigree master.

In the early 1800s, Norway (previously governed by Denmark) celebrated the signing of the Constitution of Norway by initiating a movement to develop a unique Norwegian identity. Key to that movement was developing a distinctive style of dress, similar to the Arab burnoose or German lederhosen. Men, women, and children wear bunads, Norway's national costumes, on special occasions such as weddings, baptisms, and festivals. People also wear the costumes on Norway's National Day, the 17th of May (the day the constitution was signed, equivalent to Independence Day in the United States).

Typically made of fine woolens and soft cottons,

11–12 Some sølje pieces are oxidized, allowing details to pop.

13-19 Jewelry artist Lisa Gallagher, based in Pennsylvania, does filigree based on the Russian style. Note her use of filigree as a filler within a larger framework. Photos by Lisa Gallagher.

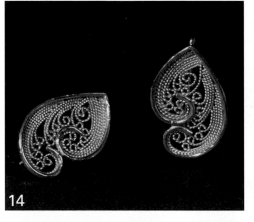

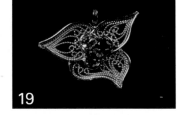

bunads are always augmented with silver accessories, such as brooches, cuff links, earrings, belts, and more. The national costume varies from district to district, and some sources suggest that there are as many as 200 different bunads—all with intricate embroidery and filigree jewelry to match. The cut of a jacket or skirt may be enough to identify a specific district, as may a bunad's embroidery or the silver that accompanies it.

Modern Norwegian filigree work is known as sølje (meaning "silver"), which became very popular with the national costume movement and continues to this day. I demonstrate the sølje technique in this book.

Russia

Like Norway, Russia also has a history of filigree work, although not all of what you see coming from Russia today is sterling silver. (Many artists use German silver, which is a nickel rather than silver alloy.) The Russian style tends to use filigree units as more of a filler element than the Norwegian style. You can apply the techniques in this book to make filigree similar to the Russian style, particularly if you have a piece that would benefit from filler ornamentation.

Asia

Asia has a long history of filigree work. Asian filigree is often very delicate and made of fine silver (999 parts per 1,000, or 99.9% pure), which makes it very

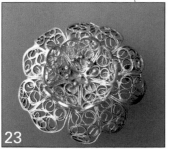

20

21

22

23

24

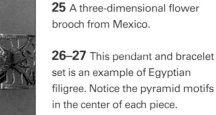

25

27

26

28

29

20 Findings and beads similar to these are widely available in many bead shops.

21–22 These pieces, both from Bali, feature very different motifs.

23–24 Delicate brooches in the Malaysian filigree tradition.

25 A three-dimensional flower brooch from Mexico.

26–27 This pendant and bracelet set is an example of Egyptian filigree. Notice the pyramid motifs in the center of each piece.

28-29 A filigree pendant and flower bracelet from Israel.

soft. Asian artisans construct many three-dimensional pieces made from very fine wire—much finer than what we'll be using for these projects. Of course, labor costs are much lower in Asia, particularly in Bali, which produces a lot of popular findings, clasps, and jewelry, often done on sterling-silver sheet. Such labor-intensive handcrafting as filigree work is still affordable, at least to those in the West. You'll find the examples of Balinese filigree shown above familiar, since many beading and jewelry shops stock Bali beads and findings.

Mexico
A strong tradition of filigree work exists in Mexico, as well as some regions of South America. As in parts of Asia, wages in Mexico are lower than in the United States, making such handcrafted artwork affordable.

The Middle East
Some Middle Eastern countries are known for their incredible metalwork and low labor prices. I've heard several stories of people going to markets and mainly paying mostly for the metal, not the work. Israel, Yemen, Turkey, and Egypt are among the countries that have a strong filigree tradition in the Middle East; two examples of Israeli filigree are shown above. Many Jewish religious artifacts are decorated with silver filigree as well.

India
In India, the filigree art form has been practiced since

30

31

32

33

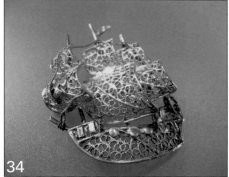

34

35

36

37

30 A small hinged purse necklace, representative of Indian filigree. Larger examples can be extremely detailed and sculptural in nature.

31–32 Pieces by Italian artist Vincent Sorrentino (also known as Sorrento). He immigrated to New England in 1911, started his own company, and became highly regarded for his filigree.

33–34 A butterfly and a sailing ship from Portugal; note the use of gold vermeil.

35 An intricate bracelet from Morocco.

36–37 These two rings were purchased in Senegal, but made by Maurs from Mauritania.

ancient times. Alexander the Great, who lived from 356–23 BC, invaded much of the world, including India and Egypt, which led to the craft coming to Greece and other parts of the Mediterranean. No doubt the Vikings then brought it from one of their many raids or trading trips to other parts of Europe, helping spread the art form.

In modern India, the region known as Orissa is famous for its intricate filigree creations, including fantastic, three-dimensional sculptures of boats, buildings, flowers, and other objects done in hair-thin, fine silver.

Italy

Italy has always had a strong metalworking history. Perhaps its culture and its prox-

imity to Greece—a country of equal impact on humanity and the arts—have made it a center for the jewelry world. One difference is that Italian artists work with both silver and gold (silver filigree is more common in other countries, with the exceptions of Portugal and Africa).

Portugal

Filigree in this country stems from the Moorish occupation of Portugal in the 8th century. Traces of filigree have been found in Portugal as far back as the Iron Ages. The city of Viana Do Catelo is famous for its fine filigree. Often done in silver, Portuguese filigree is sometimes given an overlay of fine gold. Many jewelers also work

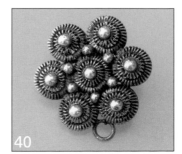

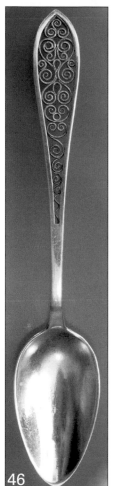

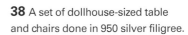

38 A set of dollhouse-sized table and chairs done in 950 silver filigree.

39 A brooch from Scotland (exact origin unknown).

40–43 A brooch, pendant, earrings, and necklace, all of unknown origin.

44 A spoon handle filled with filigree.

45 A delicate linked filigree bracelet.

46 A spoon with a filigree handle, purchased at an open market in London.

47 A dollhouse-sized filigree cabinet with hinged, movable doors.

48 A charming filigree flower brooch, ornamented with pearls.

directly in gold and make gemstone-encrusted filigree pieces. Butterflies, flowers, roosters, and sailing ships are common themes in Portuguese filigree.

Africa

Several countries in Africa (particularly North Africa, along the Mediterranean coastline) make intricate silver filigree, and some even work in gold. This influence may come from sources such as Egypt or Israel, or perhaps it's a result of Greek and Roman forays into Africa.

Origins Unknown

As an artist, I find it hard not to collect what I love to make. Shown on p. 13 are a few pieces of interesting filigree I have in my personal collection. The origins of these pieces are unknown, but they are worth looking at for artistic and construction ideas. In addition to wearable items, the collection includes practical yet decorative items, such as spoons with filigree handles.

FILIGREE VARIATIONS AND LOOKALIKES

Other techniques can create a filigree-like look. The following section shows examples of those techniques and discusses the differences between traditional filigree and these filigree lookalikes. If you enjoy doing the projects in this book, you may want to try these techniques.

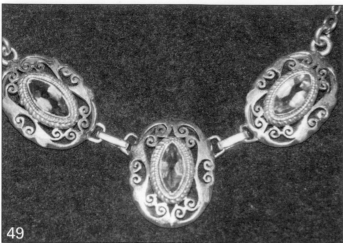

49

51

52

50

53

54

49 This piece was produced by jeweler Gillan Bradley using the piercing technique. Photo by Gillian Bradley.

50 Plique-à-jour butterflies by Linda Shores Caristo, Asheville, North Carolina. Photo by Linda Shores Caristo.

51–52 A Norwegian child's sølje brooch shown front and back; the round base is a stamped piece of sheet made to resemble traditional handmade filigree.

53–54 Additional pieces of stamped filigree in varying styles.

Piercing

Piercing is another way to form a filigree pattern that is, in some ways, the opposite of the technique featured in this book. With traditional filigree, you take pieces of wire, shape them, and put them together. Piercing, on the other hand, involves taking a plate of metal, drawing a filigree pattern, drilling holes, and sawing out the empty spaces in the pattern to leave behind the filigree pattern. The piercing technique creates a filigree design, but without the twisted wire texturing. It requires a good eye, a steady hand with a saw, and a lot of patience.

Plique-à-jour

Plique-à-jour is a variation on piercing where the pierced filigree is filled with transparent enamels. This technique produces the look of fine stained glass on a very small scale. It was very popular in the late 1800s and early 1900s. Norway's David Anderson, among others, did exquisite, high-end plique-à-jour in the late 1800s. In some ways, plique-à-jour is nearly a lost art, with few modern practitioners. It is time-consuming, with the extra step of precisely applying filigree in the small compartments between the wires and firing. Plique-à-jour can be done using filigree techniques similar to those in this book.

Stamped Filigree

Stamped filigree involves a mechanical process that literally cuts out a premade pattern from a piece of plate metal. It is essentially the

55

56

57

58

59

55–58 Various examples of cast filigree. Some of these designs make attractive cameo settings.

59 This piece features the highly polished points of diamond cutting.

mass-production form of piercing. You will often see brass filigree components made this way. Patterns are usually made with small coils of wire and granules, which are stamped onto sheet silver. Many pieces of costume jewelry and base-metal filigree findings are created from inexpensive stamped metals such as nickel and brass.

Cast Filigree

Most filigree sold in shops is either cast filigree or its variant, diamond-cut filigree. The process for both involves making an original model, either in metal or wax, and casting molten metal into a plaster mold of the model. This technique is also used for mass production. Many of these designs are of heavier construction than tradi-

tional filigree; fine filigree does not cast well because of mold shrinkage. Models can be made of pieces featuring finer filigree, but they require a mold material that makes true-size copies (for minimal shrinkage) as well as casting wax, which does not shrink and is flexible. Brittle injection wax will break when removed from rubber or silicone molds, because it is too

delicate to handle the stress of flexible molds. If you decide to try casting pieces, I recommend blue plast-o-wax and silicone mold rubber.

Diamond-cut Filigree

"Diamond-cut" is a term heard quite often these days. This variation on cast filigree starts out with the artist casting a design. Then, while

60

61

62

60–63 These wire-wrapped pieces were made by wire jeweler Helen Goga. Photos by Helen Goga.

64 Metal clay syringe pendant made by Barbara Craker; its fine lines look similar to those of filigree.

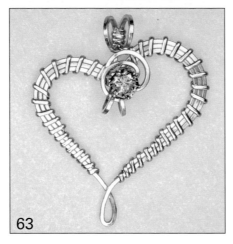

63

64

cleaning and polishing the piece, the artist takes a diamond bur and makes small nicks in the piece, which creates highly polished points that make the piece glitter in the light. A diamond-cut piece also can be used as a model and cast again. The "second-generation" piece will have a similar look, but will lose some detail because of the copying effect.

Wire Wrapping

This technique, which does not require any soldering or sawing, has gained popularity in recent years. Many people refer to it as filigree because it is made with wires and has a similar look to true filigree. It is not filigree as defined in the traditional sense, but it can be nearly as intricate and beautiful if done well.

Metal-clay Filigree

In recent years, jewelry-makers have added a new material to their repertoire: metal clay. A moldable, easily manipulated material, metal clay is shaped, dried, sanded and refined, then fired in a kiln or with a torch. The clay particles burn away, leaving behind the silver particles and creating pieces that are 99.9% pure silver. (Gold metal clay is also available.) Silver metal clay comes in several forms, including lump, paste, and sheet. It also comes in syringe form, which works much like a miniature syringe. The artist can extrude metal clay with the syringe, creating fine lines very similar to filigree. Excellent hand control is necessary to produce quality results.

metalwork

BASICS

Coil wire before annealing to ensure even heating.

I once knew a seasoned benchwork goldsmith who told me he wouldn't even touch filigree work: "Too hard," he said. Yet I had no working knowledge of silversmithing before I sat down with a torch, some tools, some filigree wire, and someone to teach me. You do not have to be a seasoned jeweler to do filigree work, as long as you are willing to try.

As in all crafts, however, understanding some basic concepts and terms before jumping into the projects will hold you in good stead. If you have previous silverworking experience, skip this chapter or read it as a refresher.

UNDERSTANDING METAL

Silver and gold in their pure forms are very soft and malleable—too soft to make them practical to be used as jewelry on their own.

Therefore, they are alloyed (mixed) with other metals to make them stronger and more durable. The silver used to make filigree varies depending on the artists and their locations. Scandinavian artists, for instance, typically use 830 silver, whereas 999 silver is used in many parts of Asia. The numbers refer to the quality of the silver and reflect the actual silver content of the wire; 830 silver is 83% silver and 17% other metals, such as nickel, zinc, copper, etc., whereas 999 silver is 99.9% silver (also called fine or pure silver). The higher the number, the softer and more ductile the wire—and thus the finer the threads that can be made and used in a design. In the case of silver, the most common combination is 925 parts of silver and 75 parts of copper per 1,000 parts. I recommend using 925 silver to make the projects in this

book, for two reasons. First, the cost of sterling-silver wire is less prohibitive than for fine-silver wire. Second, the addition of other metals (typically copper) creates a stronger wire, which will withstand wear and tear better than fine silver.

When first alloyed, metal is still relatively soft. This is because the silver and copper molecules are evenly distributed. If the silver is then worked, either by drawing it into a wire form or hammering, rolling, or bending, for example, the molecules are jammed together and the material becomes less flexible. It is thus called workhardened wire. Sometimes this is desirable, and sometimes not. Work-hardening wire is what gives it its springiness, something that is necessary when making filigree shapes.

Sometimes, however, the wire needs to be softened

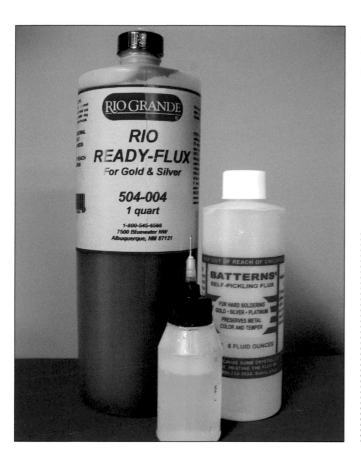

Commercially available liquid fluxes, and the bottle I use to dispense flux.

BAKING SODA

This common household product is something you should always have on hand when working with acid because it works as a neutralizer. Put some in your rinse water to make sure that any acid you transfer from the acid bowl to the rinse bowl on your piece is neutralized. You should also keep it on hand in case of spills or splatters. It may be the only thing that saves your favorite pair of jeans from looking like it's been invaded by a flock of moths!

again after work-hardening in order to continue shaping the filigree. Softening wire or metal is done by a process called annealing, which involves heating the metal to a temperature just below its melting point and then cooling it. These changes in temperature allow the recrystallization of the metal molecules, which puts them back to their original even distribution, thus making the metal soft again.

Making Wire

So how is wire made from silver? First, molten silver is poured into a form, making bars. Second, the bars are run through a rolling mill multiple times, gradually getting thinner and thinner. (A rolling mill is a machine that has two metal rollers, with either progressively smaller grooves on one or both rollers; or both rollers can be smooth, to flatten rather than form. Some rollers contain patterned grooves for producing patterned wire.) Third, the metal must be annealed (heated) periodically after one or more passes through the rolling mill, since it becomes less pliable as it is compressed by the rollers. Some metals, such as brass (an alloy of copper and zinc), must be annealed after each pass through the mill as they work-harden quickly.

A rolling mill can make the wire only so fine. After the mill has reached its limits, the wire can be made finer (smaller in diameter, or gauge) by being pulled through a steel draw plate. The draw plate features holes of nearly every gauge; a strand of wire is essentially forced into a hole and pulled, or "drawn," through the hole, which condenses and stretches the wire.

As with the rolling mill, pulling wire through a draw plate also work-hardens the metal, so the wire likewise must be annealed periodically. However, once the wire is thin and long, it becomes hard to heat evenly. When you need to anneal thin wire or a long length of wire, it is best to coil it together before attempting to anneal it. This allows the wire to be heated more evenly. If you don't coil it, you risk melting the delicate wire as well as having stretches of wire not properly annealed, which may be too stiff to bend or shape properly.

While most beginners will not need to draw down wire (make it thinner), the explanation of the process will come in handy when making filigree wire from round wire.

Annealing Metal

Annealing can be done by heating metal in a kiln or by using a torch. Since most people do not have access to a kiln and the torch method is faster, I'll explain how to use the torch. Heat sheet metal or wire by moving the torch flame along the length of the piece until you see a slight red glow in the metal. Once you see the glow, you have annealed the metal and should stop the heat. The piece must then be quenched in pickle and rinsed. (Pickle is an acid mixture that removes the dark oxidation that forms on metal during the heating process.) Once the metal is annealed, you can continue to roll or draw it until it becomes work-hardened again. Repeat the cycle as often as necessary.

CHEMICALS

When working with metals, a number of chemicals are needed for annealing, soldering, patinating, and polishing your work. Following is a brief outline of the chemicals

The needle-like tip of my flux bottle allows easy application.

you will need to have on hand. As with all chemicals, be sure to follow the manufacturer's recommended safety precautions.

Flux

Flux is a chemical used to clean silver and allow solder to flow easier and stick to the silver. It is usually based on a borax solution or boric acid solution. It is applied before soldering, which helps prevent oxidation of the metal during the heating process. (Flux also prevents firescale, which is a more extreme form of oxidation where some of the copper in sterling silver comes to the surface, leaving a red stain.)

Flux is usually used in a liquid or paste form, though some powdered flux can be used as well. I find the liquid easier to use with

wire; you can order a commercially available flux such as Battern's from a jewelry supply company. If you want to make your own, mix boric acid and water or even boric acid powder and denatured alcohol. A mixture with denatured alcohol is useful because you can burn off the liquid quickly, leaving a thin coat of flux on the wires. The advantage of denatured alcohol over water-based fluxes is that the latter can bubble up during heating as the water evaporates, which may displace wires from their positions. Even if you use a commercial liquid flux, you can add up to ⅓ denatured alcohol to the flux.

With some silverwork, you can use a brush to apply flux, but with filigree, the brush will move the wire elements. A good dispenser is a soft plastic bottle with a fine, needle-like dispenser tip. You can buy these through

a supplier, or you can make one yourself, from an empty nasal spray bottle with a metal syringe tip mounted in the opening. A little silicone or epoxy will seal the connection between the bottle and the tip. The flux can then be applied drop by drop or in a stream to the entire piece without disturbing your layout.

As with any chemicals you heat, be sure to have good ventilation so that you do not breathe more of the fumes than necessary.

Pickle

Pickle is an acid mixture that is used to remove the oxidation that forms on silver during the heating process. This oxidation usually takes on a blackish or reddish coloring (red coming from the copper in the alloy). Silver is much more prone to oxidation than gold. With gold, it is often

sufficient to pickle only when you are finished with the piece. Silver, however, oxidizes every time you solder it. To ensure clean solder joints, you must pickle the piece in the acid solution after each soldering session to remove the oxidation.

As pickle is an acid, you have to take certain precautions. Store the pickle in a glass container, ideally one you can cover when not in use. While regular glass is usable, heat-resistant glass such as Pyrex is preferable. Because hot pieces of silver are likely to sizzle and splatter when put into a cool liquid, make sure your bowl or jar is high enough to catch splatter. (I don't know how many holes I put in my blue jeans the first years I worked with filigree because I wasn't careful enough!) When taking objects out of the pickle, always use either copper or stainless steel tweezers. Car-

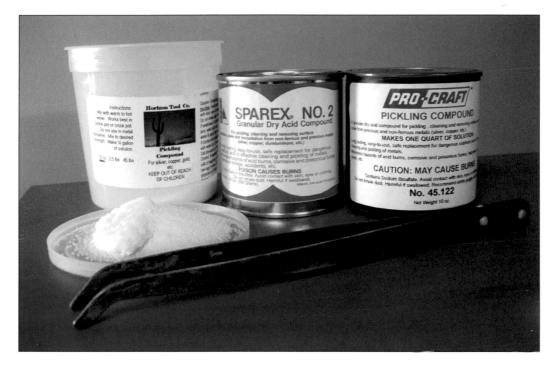

LIVER OF SULFUR

Silver will oxidize on its own over time, creating a darker hue on the silver. Sometimes it can be desirable to speed this effect and achieve it without the lapse of time. While I don't use this with my filigree work, it can add contrast to a pattern (see the example of the oxidized sølje on p. 10).

To make a liver of sulfur solution in which to dip your pieces of silver, mix chunks of dry liver of sulfur (available through jewelry supply companies) with warm or hot water; the resulting liquid should develop a greenish-yellow tinge. Dip your silver pieces in the warm solution for a few seconds, then dip into cool water to stop the oxidation. Dry your piece. Repeat this process until you have achieved a level of patina that pleases you. Excess patination can be polished away, leaving the oxidation only in the nooks and crannies of the piece. Intense oxidation can be achieved by heating the piece and dipping it in the solution while still warm.

bon steel will break down in the acid and enter your acid solution, which will contaminate it and leave a layer of rust on your silver when you put it in the pickle.

Most pickle for silver is based on a sulfuric acid mixture. When I started, I used watered-down muriatic acid, which is based on hydrochloric acid. This works in a pinch but the fumes can rust your iron tools if you keep them nearby. I prefer buying commercially available pickles such as Sparex or the equivalent—they are safer to mix and use. They usually come in granular form and can be added to hot water without danger.

If you do choose to mix your own pickle, please remember that acid and water have to be mixed very carefully. You must always add acid to water, and *never* add water to pure acid! Mixing acid and water causes a heat reaction. If you add acid to water, your acid concentration starts low and the heat reaction is slow. But if you mix water into pure acid, it can lead to such a rapid heat reaction that it quickly becomes explosive—shattering the glass you are mixing in and covering you and your surroundings with acid. This is a good reason to use heat-resistant glass. Plus, a small Pyrex bowl of pickle can be heated to improve the deoxifying reaction.

Should you spill acid or splatter it on yourself or your clothes, rinse the exposed area vigorously with cold running water. Always keep a box of baking soda handy; baking soda neutralizes acid, and applying it to the spill or exposure can prevent damage. Baking soda also can be used to neutralize old or contaminated pickle before disposal. (Be sure to follow the manufacturer's guidelines for disposing of pickle.)

This brings us to the next step: After dipping your hot silver in pickle, you don't want to handle it with acid on it, so it has to be rinsed. Therefore, keep a second bowl on your bench with water in it, and mix some baking soda into this water to help neutralize the acid. (If you don't do this, you have to be sure to change your rinse water often, as the acid content will slowly increase with the rinsing of each piece.) If you do use baking soda, the solution will gradually turn more and more light blue. This means that copper molecules are building up in the solution. When you rinse the piece in the baking soda solution, you should see a slight bubbling. This is the baking soda neutralizing the acid. If you no longer see this reaction, it means your

This is the basic layout for an area to solder at your bench. You'll need a torch, soldering brick or tripod, and two containers (one to pickle and one to rinse).

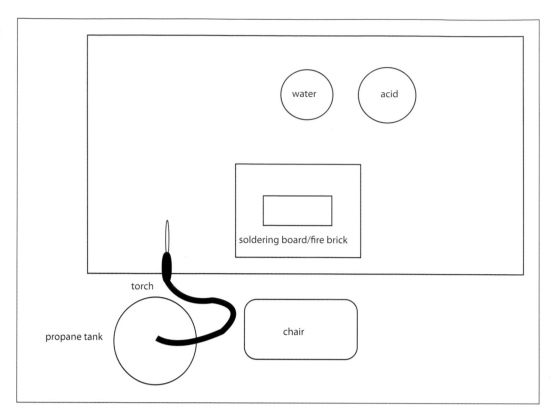

water

acid

soldering board/fire brick

torch

propane tank

chair

baking soda is spent—either get a fresh bowl of water and baking soda, or just add a little more baking soda.

Buffing and Polishing Compounds

You will need certain basic compounds for polishing your work to give it a high shine. Buffing compounds such as tripoli or white diamond will remove scratches and other imperfections; white diamond or the equivalent is somewhat less greasy and messy than regular tripoli. Red rouge, Zam, and Fabuluster are several common polishing compounds, although red rouge is more suitable for use with gold because of its rich color. Remember to use good ventilation and a dust collector and mask when polishing. After polishing, you need to clean your pieces. You can buy commercial ultrasonic chemicals, but you can also use a strong dish detergent with some ammonia added. This cuts through the fats left behind from the polishing compounds. The cleaning solution should be used hot, unless your piece includes a heat-sensitive stone such as an opal.

We will go into more detail on polishing on p. 41.

SOLDERING

Now that we've gone over the chemicals used in metalworking, I'll describe how they are used during the soldering process. Refer to "Tools and Supplies," p. 23, for more information about choosing a torch and a type of solder (I use sheet solder cut into small chips).

To solder pieces together, begin by fluxing the pieces with liquid flux. Place chips of solder on the points at which the pieces touch **[A]**. Light your torch and move the flame around the exterior of the piece so that the whole piece gets warmed first **[B]**, then focus your flame on the solder joints **[C]**. The ideal part of the flame to use is just beyond the most visible (bright blue) part of the flame. The solder should melt quickly and flow into the joint. Remove the flame and turn off the torch. Use tweezers to lift the still-hot piece and quench (or submerge) it in pickle for a few seconds; you can leave it in longer if there is heavy oxidation. Rinse afterward **[D]**.

tools
AND SUPPLIES

1 My current torch. Note the pencil or pen tip and the small size.

2 Use roundnose pliers to shape wire.

3 Flatnose pliers are for bending and straightening wire.

4 These elongated pliers work well for anchoring wire and working with flatnose pliers to open jump rings.

When I first began making filigree, I had extremely basic tools. While it is ideal to have certain tools, there are always creative solutions if you cannot find or afford them. The filigree wire itself is the hardest to find, as it is not generally available in the United States. In this chapter, I'll give you a few options for making wire similar to the traditional Norwegian filigree wire that I use.

TOOLS

Local hardware stores and even auto parts shots have basic tools. Beading and craft stores often stock some of the smaller items, such as pliers and cutters. Plenty of suppliers also sell specialty tools to hobbyists at reasonable costs; many of them offer phone and online ordering.

Here are the basics you will need to begin filigree work and complete the projects in this book.

Torch

A basic hardware store propane torch with a hose and small (pencil or pin) tip **[1]** is the perfect choice for filigree work—and it's relatively inexpensive. With a standard propane torch, you can solder more than one joint at a time, and heating the whole piece or a larger area is more efficient than it would be with a mini torch. Standard propane torches are readily available at hardware stores and big-box home-improvement stores. These torches use disposable canisters of propane and do not require expensive regulators.

Heat-resistant Soldering Surface

You will need something to solder on that is heat-resistant. Some choices include charcoal blocks, commercial soldering pads, and firing bricks (used to line fireplaces). The most important thing is that the option selected does not break down easily from repeated heating, which can cause a bumpy surface. Filigree depends on having an even surface for laying out the pieces. I do not recommend magnesium blocks; they tend to break down quickly and bubble up, displacing the silver units. I use a firebrick. You may also want to use a larger ceramic tile under your soldering block to catch stray heat and prevent burning your bench.

Pliers

You will need at least two pairs of pliers: a flatnose jewelry pliers (without teeth), and a fine roundnose pliers. Roundnose pliers **[2]** are used most when shaping filigree wire. The finer the tips are, the tighter the curls and better control you have of your shapes. Flatnose pliers **[3]** are used for making sharp bends and straightening out wire if necessary.

I also recommend cable-nose pliers **[4]**, which are basically elongated pliers. Naturally, having extra pliers of different sizes on hand is also helpful, such as an extra pair of flatnose pliers for closing jump rings.

Cutters

You will need wire and sheet cutters. The wire cutters can be either side **[5]** or end cutters and do not need to be heavy because the majority of the wire you will cut is 1mm or less in thickness. The sheet cutters or shears **[6]** can be used to cut sterling plate for cabochon backings (though saws are preferable), but will be used primarily to cut solder chips from solder sheet.

Tweezers

At least three kinds of tweezers are needed for working with filigree. First, you will need a pair of soldering tweezers. I prefer the self-locking, bent-tip kind **[7]** with fiber grips. These tweezers are useful in a number of situations, especially if you need to hold a piece in place while soldering. Buy the stainless-steel type; it's worth the extra cost as you can also use stainless in your pickle. Second, you will need a pair of fine-tip tweezers **[8]** for picking up and placing solder where it needs to go on the design. You'll also need pickle tongs, which are usually made of copper. (You can substitute stainless-steel tweezers, but not standard steel as they will be attacked by your acid and contaminate it with iron molecules. Once contaminated, the pickle will leave iron stains on any silver placed in it.)

Solder Pick

One very handy tool to have is called a solder pick **[9]**. It is worth investing in and learning how to use. It allows you to lift and transport solder from your soldering surface to your piece, nudge

5 I recommend medium-weight side cutters.

6 Metal shears are used primarily for cutting solder.

7 Self-locking tweezers with fiber grips are priceless in this work.

8 Fine-tip tweezers are ideal for grabbing small chips of solder.

MAKING A MEASURING TOOL

Purchase a piece of base-metal sheet, about 3–4 in. (7.6–8cm) in length **[A]**. I suggest brass, aluminum, or copper, as they are inexpensive and easy to cut. (You can find sheets of base metal at hardware stores.) Avoid steel and iron, which are difficult to cut. Use a ruler and mark off common lengths. I suggest ½ in., 1 in., 1½ in., 2 in., and 3 in. along one side. On the other side, measure out 1, 2, 3, and 4cm **[B]**. (You'll see that in the photos, the 3cm mark is missing. I didn't add this one initially, but discovered I needed it later.)

Next, cut notches in the plate with your metal shears **[C]**. At each measure mark, cut straight in about half an inch. Then cut on a diagonal to the first cut from between that measurement and the next. Repeat for all marks. Your finished piece should look something like the one below **[D]**.

At this point, you may be wondering how to use this tool. You lay the beginning of the wire at the notch for the length you wish to make. Bend the wire over the "0 point" end of the tool. Then move the bend up to the notch and do another bend at the "0 point." Because of the notch, your wire can pass through the notch, and you can make many strips of equal length. Continue bending as shown **[E]**.

The resulting wire resembles an angular coil or spring **[F]**. You then can snip the wires along each bend, giving you a bunch of pieces of approximately the same length, which you can use to make filigree shapes of consistent sizes **[G]**.

A

B

C

D

E

F

G

9

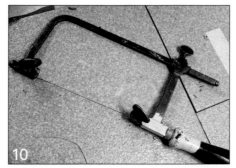

10

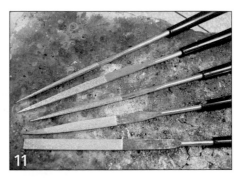

11

12

13

14

9 Use the fine point of a solder pick to lift and transport solder.

10 Use a saw to remove extra silver sheet when making cabochon settings.

11 Hand and needle files smooth filigree and metal sheet.

12 Use a solid steel ring mandrel for measuring and shaping.

13 Invest in a nylon or rubber hammer (left) as well as a polished metal planishing hammer (right).

14 A flexible shaft can be used for fine polishing, twisting wire, and wrapping wire around mandrels.

15 Instead of purchasing a professional polishing motor, you can make your own.

15

solder in the right direction when it begins to flow, and push stray filigree units into the right position.

Handsaw or Jeweler's Saw

Another hand tool that's necessary to have is a handsaw or jeweler's saw **[10]**, but if I could avoid saws, I would. I'm constantly breaking the blades in my impatience to cut out the shape. However, using a saw is the proper way to remove excess silver sheet when making cabochon settings, and should you decide to try piercing work, it's a must.

Files

You will also need needle files **[11]**, which are small files useful for tight spaces. Needle files are available in either traditional or diamond coated forms. You will mostly use the smaller files, but some larger files are good to keep on hand as well. You'll also want a few hand files for smoothing metal sheet. Buy varying degrees of shapes and coarseness— all will come in handy at some point.

Ring Mandrel

A ring mandrel **[12]** is something you may wish to invest in eventually. There are two kinds: hollow ones meant only for measuring existing

rings, and solid steel ones which both measure and serve as a specialized anvil for shaping rings.

Hammers

You will likely need two kinds of hammers **[13]** at some point: a polished metal planishing hammer for forging metal (such as hammering flat twisted wire) and a nylon or rubber hammer, preferably weighted, for shaping rings without marring the metal. An anvil or steel block is the ideal surface for hammering.

Flexible Shaft

A flexible shaft **[14]** is a rotary motor attached to a hook/holder. The handpiece

16-17 Make a dust collector from a used kitchen ventilation unit. Here are front and back views of mine.

usually has a drill-like chuck that holds small polishing and grinding tools. If you don't have a flexible shaft, you will need a hand drill with a crank. This will have two uses: twisting wire for making filigree wire, and wrapping wire around small, straight, round mandrels into coils for jump rings. (You also have the option of buying finished jump rings from a supplier.)

Cratex Wheel
A Cratex wheel is a rubberized grinding wheel that can be used with a flexible shaft tool. It contains an abrasive that will grind away unwanted lumps or scratches on silver. Use it to go over areas of square wire that need cleaning up. Keep the flexible shaft moving to keep the finish even. If you stay in one place too long, you risk digging a deeper groove in the silver. Avoid using a Cratex wheel on filigree wire unless absolutely necessary, because it can easily remove the pattern in the wire.

Measuring Tools
While you can measure each piece with a ruler or tape measure, there is a simpler way. You can make a kind of wire measuring tool or template

(see p. 26 for instructions), which will let you cut many wire strips of equal length. This is important when making pieces with repetitive sizes and shapes, as we will for the first few projects. Specific measuring becomes less critical as you develop a more intuitive approach to wire lengths and design.

Big Equipment
A rolling mill is the ideal tool to flatten wire used for filigree work. However, as this is expensive, you can make do with a planishing hammer to hammer the wire flat. It's a cruder technique that takes some practice to master, but it's how I began before I had access to a rolling mill.

You will also need polishing equipment. You can purchase a professional polishing motor, but it can be expensive. If you're not ready to invest in a polisher and suction system, you can make a polishing motor. If you have a friend with a little mechanical know-how, try to get a used washing machine motor from the dump or other source. One axle is enough, but a double axle also works well. Bolt the motor to a board and wire it to an on/off switch **[15]**. Jewelry supply houses carry tapered spindles that you can

attach to these motors.

You'll also need a dust collector **[16–17]** to keep from inhaling the microfine particles that are produced during the polishing process. Dust collectors are easy to make. Find a strong, used kitchen ventilation unit and replace the usual metal filter with a fiberglass one. Stand the kitchen vent on its back end so the filter is right behind your polishing wheel. Some used kitchen vents even have built-in lights, which come in handy when polishing.

SUPPLIES
Traditional Norwegian filigree is made from 830 or 925 quality silver. Sterling silver, or 925, is the international standard, and it's also the wire that I recommend. 925 silver is available through mail-order sources or local jewelry supply shops. However, pre-made filigree wire is not readily available in the United States, so you will have to make your own. (Although it is possible to make filigree jewelry out of non-traditional wire, the twisted, flattened filigree wire contrasts nicely with square wire, and the flat shape makes soldering easier.) See "Resources," p. 112, for a list of wire suppliers.

18

18 Use metal shears to cut a sheet of solder into thin parallel strips.

Wire and Sheet

A scale of measurement called "gauge" identifies the thickness of metal wire and sheet. The higher the number, the thinner the metal. For the projects in this book, you will need 18-gauge square wire, 16-gauge square wire, and either 24- or 26-gauge round wire or 20-gauge pre-twisted wire or filigree wire. If you are going to make a custom cabochon setting, you will need 26- or 24-gauge sterling-silver sheet, and either sterling-silver strip wire or fine-silver bezel wire.

Solder

Many kinds of solder are available. Any silver solder you buy has to be silver solder meant for use with sterling silver. Electric solder is not usable with silver as it eats away the sterling alloy. Plumber's silver solder also isn't usable.

Solder comes in various forms. I prefer sheet solder, which can be cut into small chips. Some people prefer finished mixed-paste solder, which is a mixture of powdered solder and a moist flux. It is usually applied with a fine-tip syringe. It's difficult to use on filigree because it is hard to apply without displacing your filigree pieces. It has its uses though, including attaching settings to your filigree piece and soldering hard-to-reach areas.

Solder is also available in wire form and powder form. I have never used powdered solder, but many people do. It is not as readily available as other forms, but may be worth trying. Wire solder is not recommended for filigree work, as it tends to roll off the joints too easily.

Silver solder used for making jewelry has varying degrees of hardness: hard, medium, easy, and extra-easy. This refers to the ease with which it melts. The harder it is to melt, the higher the silver content and the closer the joint will be colorwise to sterling. I usually use hard silver solder for soldering joints and medium to easy for soldering settings into place. Some metalsmiths like to use hard solder for their first joint on a piece, medium solder for the second, and easy for the third and subsequent joints. The idea is that, each time you use the torch on a piece to heat it up, you run the risk of melting previous joints. Since hard solder requires more heat to melt, a joint made with hard solder shouldn't melt while you're making another joint using medium or easy solder. How-ever, most of your soldering will be done on a flat piece, so even if a joint remelts, it should not move or loosen. If you work on more three-dimensional pieces, varying the solder hardness will be more important. Until you get used to working with fine wires, you may prefer to use medium or even easy solder and work up to using hard in the future.

When using sheet solder, you will want to cut it into small chips of solder for placement on your pieces. This is one case when you use your shears. First, you cut several thin strips parallel to each other **[18]** using shears. Use sharp shears, which will allow you to cut the strips close together. Loose or dull shears will slip on narrow strips, and you will end up cutting strips twice as wide as you need or not cutting at all.

Once you have cut a few strips of solder in one direction, take your shears and cut perpendicular to your original cuts so that you end up with small square and rectangular bits of solder. They do not need to be the same size; you will want some larger and some smaller for different-size joints.

Basically, you want an assortment of small solder chips the size of sesame seeds on up to caraway seeds or small grains of rice. Keep the chips sorted and labeled in separate containers; it's extremely difficult to tell the difference between an easy solder chip and a hard chip.

Filigree Wire

Check with silver suppliers periodically for filigree wire; better yet, request it every time you place an order for supplies or talk to your shop-keeper. Eventually filigree wire will become readily available in the United States. Until then, you may have to make your own. You can do this in several ways.

First, you can try planishing twisted wire. If you can find 22-gauge twisted wire, you just need to flatten it, either with a rolling mill or with a planishing hammer. The latter is a crude method, but the cost of a rolling mill is prohibitive to the average home jeweler or hobbyist. Hammering should be done with a polished planishing hammer using an even, medium-strength stroke on a polished anvil or steel block. If the hammered wire is too thin or uneven, it will not bend evenly and your curves will be uneven. The final dimensions of your ideal filigree wire should

19 The left wire is the finished, Norwegian-produced commercial filigree wire. The others are home-made wires. The wire third from the right is unflattened twist wire.

20 Basic steps to produce home-made filigree wire.

MAKING FILIGREE WIRE

Step 1: Fold a length of wire in two, exactly.

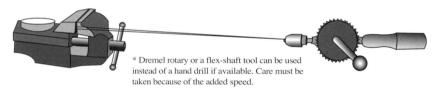

Step 2: Place the loose ends into the grip of a vice, and the folded end firmly into the chuck of a hand drill*. Hold the drill so that the wire is taught and begin turning the handcrank, twisting the length of wire. Keep taut and twist until one end snaps. **USE EYE PROTECTION!**

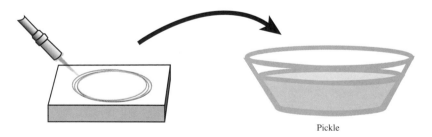

* Dremel rotary or a flex-shaft tool can be used instead of a hand drill if available. Care must be taken because of the added speed.

Step 3: Coil the twisted wire into an even bundle (keep wires close together in the loops). Anneal, pickle, and rinse. **Repeat step 2 to get a tighter twist.**

Pickle

Step 4: Run twisted wire through a flat rolling mill adjusted for approximately 0.5mm thickness. If you don't have a rolling mill, you can gently and evenly hammer the wire flat, preferably with a planishing hammer (smooth, metal hammer).

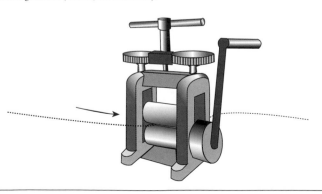

20

be around 1mm x 0.5mm for larger filigree wires; the thickness should be about half the width of your final planished wire. Once you are done with the projects in the book, feel free to experiment with different thicknesses of twisted, flattened wire in your designs.

If you cannot get pre-twisted wire, you will have to make the twisted wire yourself. Begin with a length of 24-gauge (or 26-gauge for finer wire) sterling-silver wire. If you can get it dead soft (annealed) from the supplier, that's best. Otherwise, it's a good idea to anneal it before trying to twist it.

Take a length of wire (6 ft./1.8m is a good length to start with), then double it over on itself so that it's bent in the middle and both ends come together. Put the bend of the wire in the jaws of your hand drill. Put the two ends firmly in the jaws of a vice. Walk away from the vice with the drill until the wires are taut. Before you begin twisting the wire, please remember the importance of using eye protection. When twisting wire, it often snaps when it has reached its twisting limit, and you do not want to get the end of

21 Pre-fabricated settings are available in a wide variety of styles and sizes.

a very springy wire in your face or eyes.

While keeping the wire taut, begin turning the drill. As it twists, the length of wire will be drawn shorter and shorter. Allow yourself to move forward as the wire pulls you forward, but keep the wire taut or it will twist up onto itself.

You will reach a point where either one end of the wire snaps, or the wire twists up on itself despite your best efforts. That means it's time to stop twisting. Examine your wire; if you have a nice, dense twist, where the wires are almost perpendicular to the length of the wire, then you are finished with the twisting. If the wires aren't evenly twisted or dense, you will need to make the twist tighter. Either way, the wire should be annealed at this point. If you need to make the twist tighter, then repeat the twisting process after annealing. If it is finished, then go on to the next step, which is flattening your wire.

If you have a rolling mill, flattening twisted wire is pretty simple. Set the thickness to approximately half a millimeter and run the annealed wire through the mill. It is better to err on the side

of caution and run the wire too thick the first time and run the wire through the mill twice; you cannot repair the wire if you make it too thin. If you don't have a rolling mill, you will have to use a planishing hammer and an anvil or steel block. Begin by lightly hammering one end of the wire until you get the thickness you desire. Once you have the feel for the wire and the hammer, work your way carefully and evenly down the length of the wire. It won't be as even as a rolling mill would make it, but it's usable. That's how I used to do it, and I got some wonderful results.

Please note that homemade wire can vary in appearance from batch to batch. You should try to make enough in a batch to construct an entire piece rather than switching batches halfway through. It keeps the appearance of the filigree wire consistent.

For quick reference, see **[20]**.

Findings

Filigree is a time-consuming technique. While I will try to give you a number of tips and tricks to help you save time, it still takes more time

than many other jewelry-making techniques. One way you can save time is to use prefabricated findings. If you wish to make them yourself, you may, but for the purposes of this book, it's assumed that most findings such as clasps and earring hooks are ready-made. Findings may be purchased at local bead or craft stores and through mail-order or online jewelry supply companies. See "Resources," page 112, for a list of suppliers.

Settings

You can save a lot of time by using prefabricated settings for gemstones and cabochons **[21]**. Depending on the setting type, it takes me between 15–30 minutes to make a setting. Putting that into perspective, if it takes me one hour to solder my filigree (I'm pretty fast), 30 minutes to do the setting, and 15 minutes to do the finishing, the setting takes nearly 30 percent of my work time.

Depending on the type and size of the settings, you can expect to pay between 10 cents for a small cabochon (cab) setting up to around $10 or so for larger faceted settings. On average,

you're looking at a price of about $3–$4 per setting as opposed to the $5–$10+ per setting for your time and materials. You are better off using your saved time doing more filigree work.

Of course, you cannot buy a finished setting for every stone—many are irregular in shape or size, or perhaps your design requires a custom-designed setting. In these instances, you will have to make your own settings. We will look briefly at making an irregular cab setting in Project 9 (p. 78.)

With cab settings, you will find two basic kinds of prefab settings: serrated and nonserrated. The serrated settings have a saw-toothed edge, which is easier to set than nonserrated settings. However, the serrated settings are less elegant than the nonserrated style. It's a tradeoff—ease of use versus appearance. Which you choose is a mixture of personal choice and your skill level when setting stones.

Faceted stone settings are more complicated than cab settings because you have to set the stones in prongs, which will hold them in place. This is a subject all to itself. If you are not expe-

22 The gold, spoon-shaped dangles on this piece are known as skjebladløv ("leaves" in English). They're hard to find outside of Scandinavia, so I often use freshwater pearls as dangles.

rienced with faceted stone setting, I would suggest that you consider buying either easy mount, pre-notched, or snap-set style stone settings. These are settings where a place for the stone to sit has already been made in the sides of the prongs. You will still have to do some bending and cleanup on the prongs, but you won't have to worry about filing a notch in each prong or learning how to use setting burs.

One other option for setting gems is somewhere in between a finished setting and making one from scratch. You can use something called gallery bezel—a patterned strip wire with built-in prongs that bend over the stone. You can either use a silver sheet backing, or you can make a small step on the inside of the bezel by soldering a wire on the back side of the bezel. Take your metalworking skill level into account when planning to use bezel settings.

There are many sources for buying settings; see "Resources" for a list. I also keep an eye out on eBay for bulk parcels of settings, which can be purchased for a fraction of the catalog price.

Jump Rings

Used in virtually every piece of jewelry (with the exception of rings), these handy findings can be purchased as well. You need to have jump rings that can be either soldered or are sturdy enough to hold a chain onto your designs. When I make larger necklaces, where I add a chain directly to the piece, I rarely solder the jump rings holding the chain in place. The reason for this is that if you need to polish the piece in the future, it's better to do so without the chain attached. Believe me, you don't want to get your chain caught in a polishing wheel and have your filigree dragged in and smacked against the polisher a dozen times before you can hit the off switch. It's a gut-wrenching feeling to have a piece you've just spent three to five hours making be destroyed in less than 30 seconds!

Dangles

In Norway, filigree artisans often use small, domed pieces called "leaves" as dangles **[22]**. These dangles are usually gold vermeil and either teardrop-shaped or round. Most likely, you will have to find something else to use as these are not readily found outside of Scandinavia. I often use freshwater pearls of various sizes and shapes. To attach the pearl dangles, you will either need very thin head or eye pins or to make your own ball pins from 24-gauge wire. (See Project 1, p. 46, for more details on how to make these.) Otherwise, you can use beads, charms, or anything that dangles. The filigree style is very well suited for using dangles—especially chandelier earrings with pearls or other gems hanging from the bottoms.

Other Findings

Beyond those listed above, other findings you may need include earring hooks, clasps for chains, and silver chain for larger necklaces. Earring hooks can be bought or made. Clasps and chain should most likely be purchased because making them takes a lot of time. Chain should be open enough to put jump rings through the ends for attachment to the filigree pieces. I do not recommend using solid flat chains or very heavy chains—a 1–2mm thick basic linked chain is best. For pendants, I recommend a box link chain. The patterning in the chains resembles the patterning in filigree wire.

Now you should be ready to move on to the practical part of the book: learning to make the basic filigree elements you will be using in your projects.

basics

SHAPING AND POLISHING

In this chapter, you'll learn the basics of making filigree, including creating a variety of standard shapes, making granulation for ornamentation, and polishing the metal until it gleams. The techniques learned here will provide a base of understanding for making and finishing the projects in this book.

Spend time practicing the basic filigree shapes that follow. When you are comfortable with the feel of the wire, go on to the first of the projects. Be sure to start at the beginning and work your way up to the advanced pieces. The first projects use just a couple of shapes in repetitive patterns. In later projects, I will introduce the use of square wire frameworks, settings, and more complex designs with many different filigree units, as well as asymmetrical designs.

Once you complete a project, turn to "Polishing" on page 41 for detailed instructions on giving your piece a professional finish.

SHAPING

While the actual shapes you can create with wire are nearly infinite, some basic shapes are especially useful to start with. Some of these shapes are symmetrical and some asymmetrical. Some are "single" and some are "double" shapes. Once you've mastered the art of making consistent shapes, you can make the variations you may need for other designs.

Use three tools when making these shapes: fine-tip roundnose pliers, flatnose pliers, and, most importantly, your fingers. You might think that you will do all the shaping with your roundnose pliers, but the truth is that roundnose pliers are used primarily for making the smallest part of the curls. They also are used as an anchor point for holding the wire while you use your fingers to create curves.

The wire you will use is naturally springy. It's this tension that you will guide with your fingers into the elegant curves of filigree. If you only used your pliers, you would soon find that the elegant curves would disappear in favor of a more angular and uneven appearance.

Experiment with these shapes, and don't let yourself get too frustrated when they don't come out perfectly at first. It takes time to get the feel of the wire. Use the roundnose and flatnose pliers to "correct" the pieces that do not come out the way you had planned. Do it gently, however, as sharp bends in wire are difficult to remove once you put them in.

We will start with a basic spiral and move on to what I call the "lima bean" shape and its variations, along with other symmetrical shapes. The lima bean shape will be used often in the beginner projects, so make plenty of them. You'll need them, and the repetition of making so many will help you get the necessary feel for how the wire works, how much pressure you'll need to apply, and where you'll need to apply that pressure to get the desired results.

If you want to practice without using up your silver, try making filigree wire out of 24-gauge brass wire for practice purposes only. (Although you can connect brass pieces through a process called brazing, that technique is different than soldering and is not covered in this book.)

The Basic Curl

An Italian mathematician of the Middle Ages, known then as Leonardo of Pisa, but now known as Fibonacci (from *filius Bonacci*, meaning "son of [Guglielmo] Bonacci"), found that there was a mathematical sequence that occurred as a remarkably common pattern in nature. This pattern is called the Fibonacci Sequence, in which each number is the sum of the two preceding numbers: 1, 1, 2, 3, 5, 8, 13, 21, 34, 55, 89, 144, 233, 377, 610, 987, and so on ad infinitum.

The ratio of successive pairs is called the Golden Ratio: 1.618033989, or about 1.62, and the ratio remains the same regardless of how high the numbers progress.

The Fibonacci number pattern occurs so often in nature that it is considered one of the principal laws of nature. In particular, the Golden Ratio can be seen in the proportions of the spirals on common snail shells. Basically, the distance between each part of a spiral increases by a factor of about 1.62. This pattern also shows up in other places in nature, including the number of petals on flowers and even the proportions of the bones in your own fingers.

Now, before your eyes glaze over any more, all you really need to know is that the basic curl should resemble a snail shell. I don't expect anyone to measure and calculate the distance between the coils of the curve. I do, however, want you to approach your spirals and

think, "Does this look like a snail shell?" This is a pattern that occurs over and over again in nature, and if you make your spirals in a pattern approaching the Golden Ratio, it will seem natural to the eye. If the proportion is too far off, intuitively you will see that something is not quite right.

The basic curl is achieved simply by bending the wire into a curl using roundnose pliers. There are many variations, but all your curves should resemble a snail shell.

Making a Spiral

As mentioned in the beginning of this chapter, the key to a good curve or spiral lies not in your pliers, but in your fingers and the springiness of the wire. Therefore, if you are making your own filigree wire, it is important that you do not anneal the finished filigree wire after rolling it flat.

Begin by cutting the length of wire you need for the filigree unit you want

to make. In the beginning, I recommend using the measuring tool shown on p. 26, especially if you are making a project that has many of the same pieces. As you grow in experience, you will probably do it simply by eyeing the length needed for a unit.

When you use the measuring tool, you will often see that the ends of the wire bend slightly where you bent it around the tool [1]. Likewise, when you take wire off a spool or coil of wire, it will curve in one direction. When bending wire, pay attention to these tendencies and make the curve in the same direction. Bending with the flow will make the curve more natural in appearance and you will fight less with the wire.

Start by gripping the end of the wire with the very tip of your roundnose pliers and twisting it into a nice, even center of a spiral [2].

Next, use your fingers to drag the other end of the wire around and into a spi-

ral, using the pliers more as an anchor than as a means of bending. This will give you a basic single curl [3]. If you want to make it a multilayer spiral, continue to turn the pliers while exerting pressure on the loose end of the wire until you get the desired shape.

Practice: Using the measuring tool, cut several pieces of wire at 3cm lengths. Then try to create as many basic curls resembling the ones in the picture on p. 36 as you can. Make at least 10 of them as alike as you can and set them aside for Project 7 (p. 70). Having extras is always a good idea. You never know when you will melt one and need another.

Basic curls should resemble snail shells; note the shape in both of these.

1 Note the slightly bent ends of the cut wire. Be sure to bend in the same direction when making filigree shapes; the resulting curves will have a more natural appearance.

2 Grip the end of the wire with the tip of your roundnose pliers to begin a spiral.

3 Create at least 10 curls resembling this one; you'll use them all in Project 7.

The Lima Bean

This is the first shape I learned when I began with filigree. It is the basis for several other symmetrical shapes that you will use. Begin it the same way you begin a basic curl, by gripping the ends of the wire with the very tip of your roundnose pliers. However, after making the first curl, begin at the other end of the wire and make a second curl that bends back and meets the first one. If your first few limas are lopsided **[4]**, don't worry; it may take some practice before you're able to make symmetrical limas.

Most of the projects in this book that feature the lima bean shape use wire 1½ in. (3.8cm) in length, so you should practice making limas using this length of wire. This length will give you enough maneuvering room with your pliers to make nice inner loops on each of the curls. If you have very fine roundnose pliers, try making some shapes using 1³⁄₁₆ in. (3cm) lengths of wire. This makes a smaller lima bean shape, which works well with Project 3 (p. 54), a pair of filigree earrings. The final size of the earrings varies significantly with the length of the wire chosen to make the limas, despite there being such a small initial difference between 1³⁄₁₆- (3cm) and 1½-in. (3.8cm) lengths of wire.

Practice: To make the first few projects in this book, you will need to make at least 45 lima bean units resembling the ones in **[5]**. If you feel comfortable making the smaller units, then make at least 24 using 1³⁄₁₆-in. (3cm) wire and set them aside for Project 3.

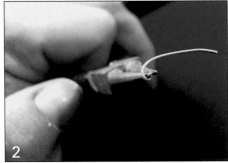

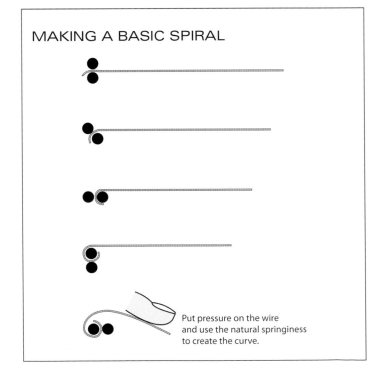

MAKING A BASIC SPIRAL

Put pressure on the wire and use the natural springiness to create the curve.

4

5

6

LIMA BEAN

MAKING A LIMA BEAN

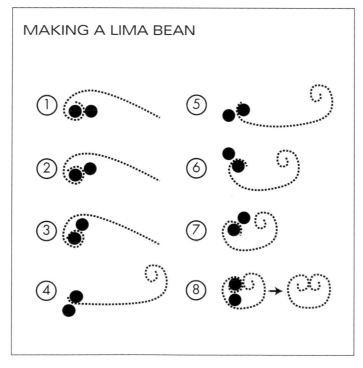

4 Bending wire takes practice. If your limas come out lopsided, simply use your pliers to correct the shape.

5 Make at least 45 1½-in. limas like this one, and set them aside for use in the first few projects.

6 The final size of finished limas varies according to the starting length of wire. These limas were made with 1 in., 3cm, and 1½-in. lengths of wire.

MAKING A HEART

HEART

7 Bend a length of wire in half, making a sharp point by pinching the bend with pliers.

8 Unfold the wire, straightening the base with the pliers.

9 The straightened wire should form a uniform V shape.

The Heart

The heart shape is very close to the lima bean shape. The difference is that you bend the wire in half before doing the curls. In some ways it's easier than the lima bean shape, because dividing it in two makes it easier to be symmetrical.

First, take a length of wire (for example, the standard 1½-in./3.8cm piece we used with the lima bean shape) and bend it exactly in half. To make a sharp point, you will need to pinch the midpoint with pliers **[7]**. You can use flatnose pliers to do this, or you can use one of my favorite tricks: Use the flat area at the base of the jaws of your roundnose pliers. This trick saves you time because you can keep using the roundnose pliers the entire time, instead of switching back and forth between pliers.

Unfold the wire partway. You may need to use your flatnose pliers to straighten the wire right at the base of the heart **[8]**. Once you have a nice V shape **[9]**, begin curling each end into spirals until they meet in the middle, creating a heart.

MAKING A WITCH'S HAT

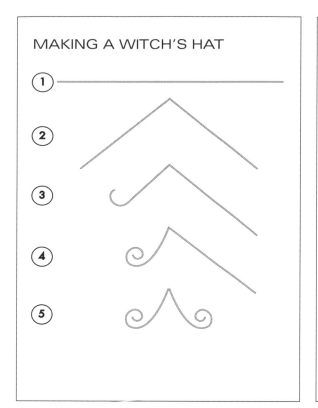

①
②
③
④
⑤

CONNECTING TEARDROPS

When you have to solder a teardrop's point to another piece of silver, end the wires at the same place.

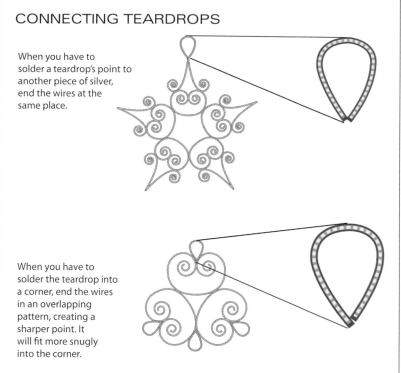

When you have to solder the teardrop into a corner, end the wires in an overlapping pattern, creating a sharper point. It will fit more snugly into the corner.

WITCH'S HAT

10

11

TEARDROP

The Witch's Hat

Begin this shape the same as the heart, but instead of bending the curls in toward each other, bend them out [10]. Keep the curls as symmetrical as possible. Use 1½-in. (3.8cm) strips of wire for slightly larger shapes and 1³⁄₁₆-in. (3cm) strips for smaller, tighter shapes.

Practice: Using 1½-in. (3.8cm) lengths of wire, make several witch's hats resembling the one in the illustration above. Make at least five of them as alike as possible and set them aside for Project 2 (page 50).

The Teardrop

This is the simplest shape, but a very important one. It is used to finish off where other shapes meet, and to make loops for dangles to hang from.

Use your roundnose pliers for this shape as a sort of mandrel rather than as pliers. Wrap a short length of wire around one jaw of the pliers until you form a teardrop. I typically use about 1cm lengths of wire for my teardrops, but you can make larger teardrops using longer wire. There are two different ways to finish off a teardrop, depending on what you are going to use it for. Over-

lap the end of one wire to another if you are going to place it in a corner, where a sharp point is needed. (This is much easier than filing tiny wires to fit into tight places.) If you plan to solder the teardrop to another piece of silver, then end it evenly or parallel. Don't worry if they don't fit perfectly into corners; there's a solution for that one coming up!

Practice: Using about ³⁄₈-in. (1cm) lengths of wire, make about 20 teardrops [11]. You will need at least 16 teardrops with overlapping ends to complete Project 1 (p. 46).

10 Your finished witch's hats should resemble this piece.

11 Make an assortment of teardrops and set them aside for upcoming projects.

SPIRAL VARIATION

WITCH'S HAT VARIATION

HEART VARIATION

LIMA BEAN VARIATION

Variations on a Theme

Most other shapes are variations on the basic shapes described in the previous pages. Some are double shapes such as double spirals, where you bend the wire at some point other than the middle and make two spirals of differing sizes. Others are variations on the heart or witch's hat shapes where the lengths and spirals are uneven. I also use variations on the lima bean shape; instead of bending the spirals toward the center of the wire, I bend them backward. (This shape works well with a silver ball in the center.)

Putting the Granulation in *Filigran*: Making Silver Balls

In Norwegian, the word for filigree is *filigran*. If you go back to the Latin, *fili* means wire and *gran* refers to the granules or balls that often adorn the designs. I find that the balls serve three purposes:

• They add decoration.

• They cover up solder joints where several wires come together or where a messy solder joint may be.

• They add strength to critical points such as where the bail attaches to the body of the jewelry.

But where do we get the little balls to put on the filigree? Why, we make them (see below for instructions). If you have any scrap silver such as cut-offs or pieces gone wrong, this is a perfect use for them. If you don't have any scrap silver, use little pieces of the least expensive silver wire you have. You can also buy casting grain, which is usually melted and poured into a mold.

MAKING FILIGRAN

Lay a silver scrap on your firebrick, flux it, and then melt it with your torch. It will form a rounded ball shape. Once you have melted one, move on to the next piece of scrap and keep going until you have done all of the scraps on your firebrick **[A-B]**. If you have a piece that is large and you want to turn it into two smaller ones, you can use your solder pick to divide it once it begins to melt, but before it becomes truly molten. I don't find it necessary to pickle the balls, so after they're melted, just let them cool on the brick, and then gather them and set them aside. I recommend making several dozen of these ahead of time in a variety of sizes. Use a hard soldering surface such as a firebrick or ceramic soldering pad, as the hard surface will make the backs of the balls flat **[C]**. This makes them much easier to place on your filigree design than if they were rounded on the back side.

12 Add a steel brush (left) to your flexible shaft tool to burnish the metal. Once finished, use a Cratex wheel (right) for further burnishing.

POLISHING

The goldsmith who taught me finishing and polishing told me that it takes him three months to properly train a polisher. As you can imagine, this is a subject for an entirely separate book. In the section that follows, however, you will learn enough basic information about finishing filigree to polish the projects in this book. I'll also give you some options for how to do the final polish.

Preparing Your Pieces

As you'll see in several of the projects, you don't go straight from the bench to the polisher. You must first prepare your pieces for polishing by following these steps:

1. Pickle the finished piece until all the oxidation has disappeared.

2. Use a steel brush attachment with your flexible shaft tool **[12, left]** to burnish the metal. Be sure to get into all the nooks and crannies around the silver balls and curls. Use a steel brush and elbow grease if

you don't have a motorized tool. Don't use a brass brush on filigree.

3. Use a Cratex wheel **[12, right]** (described in "Tools and Supplies," p. 23) or the equivalent to clean up the smooth areas of your piece, including removing excess solder and scratches. If you do not have a motorized tool, try a little 600-grit sandpaper wrapped around your fingertip or the tip of a craft stick and manually sand the areas. You may also use a file, although it can be difficult to get a stiff file to sand only the smooth areas and not the surrounding filigree. If the smooth wire is on the outside of the piece, however, you can use a file.

Polishing Equipment

You will need some kind of polishing motor. If you don't have one or cannot afford one, you can make an inexpensive one out of an old washing machine motor as discussed in "Tools and Supplies." You'll also need a dust collector or vacuum system (also discussed in the "Tools and Supplies" chap-

ter) to collect the polishing compound and silver dust that comes off of the brushes and buffs in the polishing process. Some of the compounds contain microfine particles that can be hazardous to your lungs if breathed in over a long period of time. If you can't rig a dust collector, open a window for ventilation or wear a respiratory mask such as those used by drywallers (available from your local hardware or home-improvement store). Once you have your polishing motor, round up the following items:

• A **hard felt buff:** either a standalone felt buff wheel **[13]** or a combination buff/inside ring buff **[14]**.

• A **nylon brush [15]**.

• A **cloth buff [16-17]** for tripoli or white diamond buffing compounds or the equivalent. Cloth buffs are usually stitched together so that the layers of cloth don't separate and make it too soft. (Soft and hard buffs will give you different results. A hard buff grinds away silver at a faster rate than a soft one.)

13 Begin with a hard felt buff. You can use a standalone buff wheel, or one that's combined with an inside ring polisher [14].

15 Next, use a nylon brush.

• A **soft cloth buff [18]** for polishing compounds such as red or white rouge.

• An **adapter [19]** (optional) for using flexible shaft tools on your polishing motor. This allows you to use the small tools normally used in your flexible shaft without having to physically leave the polisher and go back to the flexible shaft. This comes in handy when cleaning up prongs and difficult-to-reach areas that you may have missed earlier. This adapter usually has a small, adjustable chuck on the end to allow different-size brushes, burs, bits, and so on.

Polishing Order

The basic idea with polishing is to start with the fastest grinding tool to take away the coarsest defects. Each pass on the piece you make will smooth away smaller and smaller defects as well as different types of defects. Corrective polishing can nudge a so-so piece up a notch or two, so it's well worth learning how to properly polish your jewelry.

Polishing metal is a step-by-step process, using specific tools in a certain order. However, you will not always need to use every tool, depending on the piece

to be polished, and that is where your judgment will come in. Whether you use all or only some of these tools, you must use them in the following correct order:

1. Hard felt buff. Use this to smooth any of the nonpatterned areas of your silver, to remove larger defects in bezel settings and sheet silver, to smooth framework wire, and to smooth or shape the shanks on rings. Use to remove deep scratches or larger defects such as sharp areas that you did not remove with your Cratex wheel. Use a buffing compound such as tripoli or white diamond when working with hard felt.

2. Soft felt buff. Use this the same way as a hard felt buff, with a slightly slower cutting rate for less coarse defects. Use tripoli or white diamond with soft felt, too.

3. Nylon brush. Use on the patterned part of the wire and in and around prongs, balls, and any areas you need to get into in order to achieve a high polish. The brush will not remove the patterning on your wire unless you overdo it. Use tripoli or white diamond when using a nylon brush.

4. Hard cloth buff. Use as a final pre-polish on the smooth areas of your piece.

It cannot get into the nooks and crannies, and you should not use it with any pressure on the filigree wire or it will strip the pattern from it. Use primarily for outer, smooth frameworks and bezel settings; if your piece doesn't have such features, skip this step. Use tripoli or white diamond with a hard buff.

5. Soft cloth buff. Never skip this step. Use a soft buff with tripoli or white diamond on the whole piece, but with emphasis or pressure only on the smoother parts of the piece (framework, bezel, and so on). Use it to lightly go over the brushed filigree wire to give it a higher pre-polish shine.

6. Wash. If you have an ultrasonic cleaner, use it; otherwise, use a soft toothbrush and dish soap with a dash of ammonia to clean your piece. Thoroughly wash and dry the piece; make sure all the buffing compound and grinding debris are removed before you move on to the final polish. If you contaminate your polishing buff, it will give poorer polishing results in the future.

7. Soft polishing buff. Never skip this step. Use this buff with rouge, such as Zam or Fabuluster, and go over the entire piece. The polish-

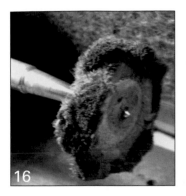

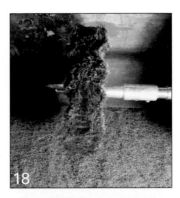

16–17 Cloth buffs are stitched together so the layers remain close and don't soften. A hard cloth buff will grind away silver faster than a soft one.

18 Use a soft cloth buff with polishing compounds like red and white rouge, Zam, or Fabuluster.

19 An adapter allows you to attach flexible shaft tools to your polishing motor.

20 Don't let your attention stray when polishing a piece. A polisher can grab and break items like this tiara faster than you'll be able to hit the off button.

ing compound does not cut or grind, only polish, so it will not hurt the patterning on the filigree wire.

8. Adapter. If needed, use around prong settings after setting the stone to get in and clean up around the tips of prongs without risking grinding them away with larger tools. It gives precision control so that you can work on small details, which otherwise would be hidden by a larger brush or buff. An adapter is also handy for hard-to-reach spots such as open areas on the inside of the framework.

Polishing Tips

Polishing is one of those techniques that's better learned by practice than anything else. Above all else, pay attention. **[20]** is an example of what happened when I let my attention stray. This is a tiara with a thin headband. I made it in 2004; it had taken nearly 15 hours to make, and I was very eager to finish it. I dropped my attention

for just a few seconds, and the polisher grabbed the tiara, broke the headband, wrapped it tightly around the spindle, and smacked the front part of the tiara on the floor of the polisher several times before I could hit the off button. Half of the filigree was intact, and the other half was sagging and mangled. I was heartbroken!

In addition to paying attention while polishing, here are a few other tips I've learned:

1. Always keep a good grip on the piece. The polishing motor will be running at 1700–3500 rpms depending on your motor. (If you use an old washing machine motor as outlined in "Tools and Supplies," note that such a motor is slower than most commercial polishers.) If you do not have a firm grip on your piece, it could be snatched out of your hand by the brush or buff and smacked into the floor or the back of the polisher. While most of the time

filigree within a framework will survive this relatively unscathed, larger pieces and fragile stones could easily be damaged.

2. Ninety percent of the time, you should hold your piece perpendicular to the brush or buff so that the brush or buff rolls over the surface of the piece and does not have an edge to snag and grab out of your hands. If you absolutely must put the edge of a piece into the brush or buff, make sure you have a strong grip.

3. If at all possible, polish any necklace before adding a chain. If you are not an experienced polisher, you risk getting the chain grabbed out of your hands and pulling the whole piece into the polisher. (This happens to experienced polishers sometimes, too.) You can also hurt your fingers if they get caught in the chain. If you have a chain that you must polish, find a piece of plastic or metal pipe and stretch the chain around that, bracing a segment top and bottom. Polish only one segment at a time, and then readjust your grip on the chain on the pipe.

4. Remember to recharge your buffs and brushes often. Before you use a buff or brush, you need to "charge" it with buffing or polishing compound. As you use it, most of that compound is shed from the buff or brush, and you have to add more. Do this with all brushes and buffs, but especially with the nylon brushes. They lose their buffing compound faster than the cloth buffs as the nylon brushes don't hold on to the buffing compound as well as the weave in the fabric of the cloth buff does.

TUMBLE POLISHING

An alternative polishing method worth mentioning is tumble polishing. Most might think of rocks when tumbling, but it's also possible to tumble-polish jewelry. This is often used in mass production when a large number of items need polishing. It's possible to do almost all of the polishing process, simply by tumbling using different media to grind down the defects in finer and finer gradations. However, what you don't have here is the control to focus on any given defect. The entire piece receives the same treatment at each stage.

I have only used tumble polishing in the final stage of polishing. Basically, I did the entire buffing process up to washing the piece before polishing. Then I put the pieces I had finished in a tumbler containing mixed stainless-steel shot, which in this case was a batch of small steel shapes ranging from round pieces to elongated pins. I then used a burnishing compound, which is basically a type of soap, sometimes containing a little citric acid, and hot water.

If you do choose to do a tumble polish for the final stage, make absolutely sure that you thoroughly clean your pieces of any buffing compound. If you put in pieces that are full of buffing compound, your final pieces will not come out bright and shiny, but steel gray.

Tumble the piece for 1–2 hours. When you remove it from the tumbler, it should have a high shine.

Advantages:
- It's time-saving when you have a lot of pieces to do.
- If you use mixed steel shot with shapes that can get into small places, it will polish inside the filigree where you cannot reach with standard brushes.
- It work-hardens your filigree by burnishing it from all sides.

Disadvantages:
- If you do the entire process by tumbling, you have less control over the removal of blemishes.
- You cannot polish your piece with all stones in place. Only hard stones such as quartz and garnets will tolerate this process. If you have a soft or delicate stone like turquoise, amber, or opal, it will not survive this process.
- Tumble polishing is not a good process for one or two pieces at a time. You can finish individual pieces faster using manual means.

If you are interested in learning more about the tumble polishing process, read the following book: *Tumble Finishing for Handmade Jewelry, 4th edition*, Judy Hoch, ISBN 0-9728269-0-4. (You can purchase this book through Judy's Web site, marstal. com.) Judy recommends using her techniques with a mild abrasive, followed by stainless steel, so as not to ruin the details in the filigree pattern.

projects

Kronesølv, or Norwegian-style Dangle Earrings

Pearl dangles ornament these traditional Norwegian filigree earrings.

The jewelry technique in this book is based on the traditional filigree work of Norway, so I'll begin with a pair of Norwegian-style earrings. Called *kronesølv* (literally, "crown-silver"), these earrings are very similar to those worn with Norwegian national costumes. Traditionally, the earrings consist of two or more trefoil-like patterns linked together and bedecked with gold-plated, spoon-shaped dangles called *skjebladløv* ("leaves" in English, referring to the leaf of a spoon). These dangles can be hard to find in the United States, so I've substituted freshwater pearls here.

YOU WILL NEED
- **12** 1½-in. (3.8cm) lima-shaped units
- **8** 1cm teardrop units
- **10** thin head or eye pins (or 24-gauge sterling-silver round wire to make eye pins)
- pair of earring wires
- **2** 4-5mm jump rings

FIGURE 1

Unless you've had previous metalsmithing experience, at this point in the book you've done very little soldering. It's always wise for beginners to have extra components on hand as they learn to solder the pieces together. Don't get frustrated if something melts, though—just fix it! Or, if you wish, you can set aside damaged units and use them to make filigran for other projects.

1 Take three of your lima bean shapes and lay them out like a trefoil, with the bottoms of the limas making a triangular shape in the middle. The three limas should be as alike in size and shape as possible **[1 and figure 1]**.

2–5 Flux the pieces with liquid flux and place three chips of solder on the points at which the limas touch **[2]**. Light your torch and move the flame around the exterior of the piece so that the whole piece gets warmed first **[3]**, then focus your flame on the solder joints **[4]**. The ideal part of the flame to use is just beyond the most visible (bright blue) part of the flame. The solder should melt quickly and flow into the joint; remove the flame and turn off the torch. Use tweezers to lift the still-hot trefoil and quench (or submerge) it in pickle for a few seconds; you can leave it in longer if there is heavy oxidation. Rinse afterward **[5]**.

FIGURE 2

Remember, when putting a teardrop into a corner, overlap the wires at the end, making a sharp point.

6–10 Select four pointed teardrops with overlapped ends to fit in the sharp corners **[6** and **figure 2]**. Once you have the four teardrops in place **[7]**, flux the piece, add solder over the joints **[8]**, and solder **[9]**. When the solder has flowed, pickle the unit while it is hot and then rinse **[10]**. You've finished the first unit!

11–12 Make three more units to match the first. You can do this in one of two ways:

• Repeat steps 1–10 three more times.

• Set up three trefoils and work on all three at once **[11]**.

If you don't feel comfortable making more than one unit simultaneously, then just make them one by one. The advantage of working up several trefoils at once is to save time. While it will take longer than doing only one, it will consume less time overall. If you choose

this option, solder one unit, then move on immediately to the next with the torch **[12]**. This way, you are only lighting up the torch a few times, rather than many times. When all the units are soldered, pickle and rinse them. You should now have four relatively similar filigree pieces.

13 It's now time to polish your pieces. You'll notice that they have a white, matte appearance. In traditional Norwegian work, they are sometimes left like this. If your pieces are not pure white, but have black or red areas of discoloration on them, heat them again, taking care not to remelt the solder, and submerge them in pickle until the discoloration disappears. If you have a pickle pot, you can use it without reheating the filigree since a pickle pot has a built-in heat source. A makeshift pickle pot can be made from a small crockpot or a coffee cup warmer and Pyrex dish.

If you want your project to have a more "finished" look, then you need to polish it further. If you have a flexible shaft tool, such as a Dremel, start by using a small, steel brush wheel and going over all the filigree **[13]**. This burnishes the silver, removing the white appearance and giving you a semi-shiny appearance. (When using one of these brushes, be sure to use eye protection. It's always good to use eye protection with rotary tools, but with this particular accessory, it's a must. These brushes frequently lose pieces of wire while in use. Since the brush is rotating, any loose pieces are thrown from the brush and can hit your eyes.)

If you are satisfied with the look of your pieces, you are finished with the polishing process. If you want to polish the piece further, use a polishing motor and the assorted buffing and polishing wheels and compounds as described on p. 44.

14 Once you have your four units polished to your satisfaction, you will need to make the dangles. If you are using freshwater pearls, as in this example, keep in mind that the holes in pearls are very small. You will need either very thin, commercially produced head or eye pins or 24-gauge sterling-silver round wire.

If you choose to use 24-gauge wire, cut several 1- to 1½ -in. (2.5–3.8cm) pieces of wire, and as we did with the granulation balls (p. 40), melt part of the wire. Focus your flame on the tip of the wire until it begins to melt. It will naturally ball up **[figure 3]**. If you do this on firebrick, however, one side will be flat and the other round. If you wish to make the ball round, hold the piece of wire vertically in your self-locking tweezers. Melt the bottom tip of the wire until it balls up at the bottom of the wire. This can happen quite quickly, so be aware of what is happening with your wire.

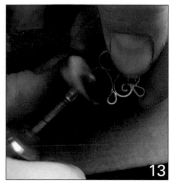

Don't forget to pickle and rinse. Clean the wires before adding the pearls, either by burnishing them or using the polishing machine.

Thread one pearl on each wire. Bend the wire around your roundnose pliers 6–7mm above the top of the pearl and thread the loose end through one of the teardrops. Continue to bend until you cross the pin with the pearl on it. At this point, you will want to neatly bend this around the pin itself in a spiral three to five times or until you run into the top of your pearl **[figure 4]**. Trim any excess and file any sharp ends. Repeat this with all three bottom teardrops on two of the filigree units, and on the outer two teardrops on the bottom of the other two units (the center

teardrop will be used to connect two pieces together).

Once you have added the pearl drops, find a jump ring 4–5mm in size. Use two flatnose pliers to open the jump ring. Put it through the middle loop on the bottom of the two-dangle piece and the top loop of the three-dangle piece. Add an earring wire to the top loop **[figure 5]**. Repeat for the other earring. The finished earrings should look like those pictured on p. 46.

Variations

Experiment with using different sizes of lima beans, as long as you use the same size limas in any given trefoil. For example, you can have a top trefoil made with 1½-in. (3.8cm) strips of wire, and make two sets of trefoils

made with about 1³⁄₁₆-in. (3cm) strips. This will give you two smaller trefoils, which you could dangle from the outer loops on the larger trefoil, as on **figure 6**.

You can also use these units to make a bracelet or as accents in a chain.

HELP! MY PIECE IS LOPSIDED!

As you solder, the force of the torch's flame can move lightweight pieces around. Before you can react, your solder may have melted, firmly connecting your piece. That's what happened with the trefoil shown here, which resulted in one lima bean being rather awkwardly connected to the other two—in other words, asymmetrical. Rather than scrapping the trefoil and starting over, use your roundnose pliers to reshape the two curled ends on the lopsided lima bean. You'll have a perfectly usable trefoil without sacrificing any silver or work.

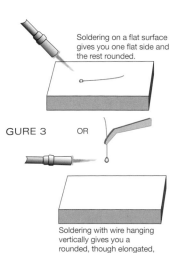

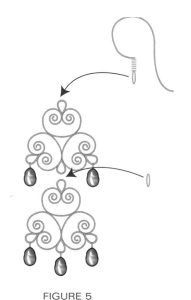

Soldering on a flat surface gives you one flat side and the rest rounded.

GURE 3   OR

Soldering with wire hanging vertically gives you a rounded, though elongated, bead on the bottom.

One of the tips of a round-nosed pliers.

Twist the loose end around the pin until you meet the top of the pearl.

Make the twist as even and neat as possible. Be sure to clip and file any loose/sharp ends.

FIGURE 4

FIGURE 5

FIGURE 6

The Star

Use basic filigree shapes to make a simple star pendant.

This project builds on the previous one, using both lima beans and a teardrop, but also introduces the witch's hat and soldering on one ball for a bit of granulation ornamentation. The project calls for 1½-in. (3.8cm) strips, but both limas and witch's hats can be done with 1³⁄₁₆-in. (3cm) strips for a smaller, tighter star.

YOU WILL NEED
- 5 1½-in. (3.8cm) limas
- 5 1½-in. witch's hats
- 1cm teardrop, with parallel wires
- 5-7mm jump ring
- 2–3mm silver ball

Is 5 Better than 3?
As in the first project, we begin with a group of limas—this time, five rather than three. It's important to choose five that are similar in size and shape so that you can make the star as symmetrical as possible.

1–3 Lay out the five limas with their backs toward the center. Make the pentagon in the middle as even-sided as you can. Flux the joints and place a solder chip on each joint **[1]**. Solder **[2]**, pickle, and rinse.

Check that each joint has soldered properly **[3]**. If they have, but the star shape is somewhat distorted, you can make small adjustments to the symmetry by adjusting the curls in or out on the individual limas. If any joints did not solder, go back and resolder those joints.

4–7 Select five matching witch's hats **[4]**. Position the five hats against each of the limas as symmetrically as possible. Because the star shape is larger than the trefoil shape you made in Project 1 (p. 46), it is more fragile. Address this issue by also soldering where the spirals meet in the center of each lima bean; this will add some much-needed stability to the overall shape. Flux the joints and place solder chips over

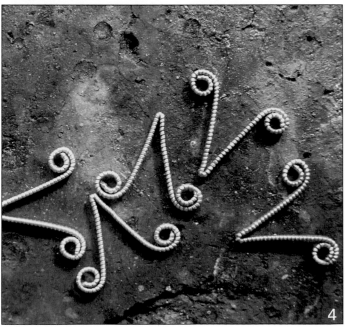

each point where the limas touch the witch's hats as well as in the middle of each lima **[5]**. If your central pentagon of limas shifted during soldering and is not totally symmetrical, compensate by adjusting the witch's hats accordingly.

When you solder this time, it's important to warm the entire piece evenly first rather than focusing on the specific joints. Do this by moving the torch in a circle, going from the outside of the piece to the inside. Focus briefly on each segment until the solder flows, then move on to the next section. Pickle and rinse the star when finished.

If you notice a joint won't solder (for example, the chip of solder gets blown away by the force of the torch), you can do one of two things:

• Solder what you can, pickle and rinse, and then solder the missing joints.

• Use a solder pick to lift a new piece of solder and place it on the missing joint while you're soldering the other joints **[6–7]**. See "How to Use a Solder Pick," p. 53, for further details.

8–9 Select one of the teardrops you made in practice, or make a new one using a strip of metal about ⅜ in. (1cm) long. Unlike the overlapped teardrops used in Project 1, this teardrop should have parallel ends to ensure that it attaches correctly to the point of the witch's hat.

Now, look closely at your soldered star **[8]**. Chances are, it won't be 100 percent symmetrical. Find the most symmetrical angle and hold the piece upright with that witch's hat pointed up. Take a flat needle file and file the tip of the upward-pointing witch's hat until it's flat, which means it will join together smoothly when soldered to the teardrop. Check the fit between the filed witch's hat and the parallel-end teardrop; both pieces should fit together smoothly with no snags or gaps at the joint. If necessary, file the ends to make it fit better.

Place the pieces on your soldering surface, flux the joint and the surrounding

area, and place a large solder chip on the joint **[9]**. Warm the surrounding area and gradually focus on the joint itself until the solder flows. Pickle and rinse.

10 The teardrop is where the jump ring will be added, so it's the point that will take the most abuse on this piece. Although adding a silver ball may seem merely decorative, it actually strengthens the joint and makes it strong enough to withstand wear and tear.

If you didn't make any practice balls, refer back to "Putting the Granulation in Filigran!," p. 40, and make some now. Make a dozen or more until you have a nice assortment from which

11

to choose. Select a 2–3mm silver ball that has a flat back, place it over the joint at the base of the teardrop **[10]**, and flux the area. Chances are, if you used a larger piece of solder when adding the teardrop, there will be enough solder in the joint to simply remelt and attach the ball to the joint without adding more solder. If not, you can always add a small solder chip.

When you begin soldering the ball into place, it will likely get shiny or even red, as if it's on the verge of melting. When the solder beneath it melts and attaches the ball to the whole piece, the shine will suddenly disappear or become more matte. Watching for this moment is something that only experience will teach you and is part of getting the feel for the metal and working with fine wires over time.

As always, pickle and rinse the piece.

11 Open a jump ring and slip it through the teardrop on top. Close it securely so that the two ends meet as perfectly as possible. Next, using the jaws of your bent soldering tweezers, lock the point in the jump ring opposite the opening. Lay the tweezers flat on the soldering surface with the points facing up.

Use your solder pick to lift a piece of solder and place it on the opening in the jump ring **[11]**. If you have positioned the jump ring correctly, the opening will be straight up and will not be touching any part of the pendant. This is important as your jump ring must hang freely; you don't want to risk attaching it to the pendant when soldering it closed.

Solder the jump ring, pickle, and rinse. If necessary, reheat and pickle to get rid of oxidation. Rinse when it has become white. Burnish with the steel brush and polish.

Variations
You can use a single star element as a pendant, or make two and leave off the jump ring to create a pair of earrings. You can even use stars as delicate Christmas ornaments!

HOW TO USE A SOLDER PICK

A solder pick is basically a long pointed tool that's used for placing, holding, and repositioning solder. Using a solder pick is a technique you should learn to do once you are comfortable with soldering filigree in general. If you are right-handed, it's advisable to learn to hold the torch with your left hand, leaving your right hand free for the fine maneuvering of the solder pick; the reverse is true if you are left-handed.

To use the solder pick, place pieces of solder on your soldering surface. Take the solder pick in one hand and the torch in the other. Hold the tip of the solder pick near a piece of solder and simultaneously heat the tip of the pick and melt a piece of solder on your soldering surface. When both are warm, touch the tip of the solder pick to the ball of melted solder, and it will attach itself without flowing or bonding to the pick. Then transport the molten solder to your piece, warm the area to be soldered, bring the pick in, and place the ball of solder on the joint. It should attach itself to the joint and flow into it.

If you can master this technique, you'll save a lot of time in the future. It will work as long as the flux hasn't burned off totally and the silver isn't too oxidized from soldering too long. If either of these is the case, try adding a little flux before using the solder pick. A note of caution, however: If you add denatured alcohol to your flux, remove the flame from the piece when you apply fresh flux or it will catch fire. Most of the time it's a small flame, but if you add a lot of flux and your face is too close, you could singe your face or set your hair on fire.

Linda's Earrings

Two basic shapes—limas and teardrops—make up these elaborate-looking earrings.

I was still in college when I came back from Norway, where I first learned filigree work that fateful summer in 1988. I made a few of the simple *kronesølv* earrings with single and double levels and showed off my handiwork.

One of my professors liked my earrings but wanted something larger. Eighteen years later, Linda still wears the pair I made for her. She is constantly telling me many people ask her, "Where did you *get* those earrings?" What else could I do but ask Linda to send me a photocopy of the earrings so that I could include the design in this book? The result is Project 3. The design uses lima beans, teardrops, and balls, and is a bit more complex than Project 1 (p. 46) or Project 2 (p. 50).

Incidentally, Linda was my first customer back before I made filigree, when I glued some quartz crystals in bell caps and she said, "If you make another pair, I'll buy them." Funny how such a small event can change your life.

1–3 Make four trefoils but do not add the teardrops. Try working simultaneously, making all four at one time, to speed production **[1–2]**. You should end up with four perfect trefoils **[3]**.

FIGURE 1

4

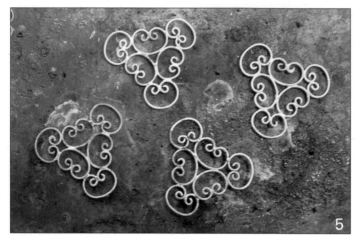

5

6

4–5 Next, take one trefoil and add on three more lima beans [**figure 1**]. Basically, you are turning around a lima bean and using it to overlap the junction between every two limas in the trefoil. Flux the pieces and add solder to all the joints [**4**], including the ones where the spirals in the center of the trefoil meet (as you did to the star in Project 2 for extra stability). Solder,

pickle, and rinse. Repeat this process with the other three trefoils to create four triangular units [**5**].

6 Now it's time to combine the triangular units. Take two of the triangles, preferably as alike as possible, and lay them down opposite each other, one pointing up and one pointing down, so that two of the outer lima beans are

touching two of the outer limas on the other unit [**6**]. Solder the two pieces together. Remember to heat the whole piece well before focusing the flames on the new solder joints.

7 You'll need one parallel-end and two overlapped teardrops for each earring, so either select teardrops from your practice pieces or make them up now. Solder the

parallel-end teardrops to the very top of the design, and the overlapped (or pointed) teardrops to the corners created by combining the triangular units [**7**]. This completes the filigree work.

8 Now, add the balls. As was the case with Project 2, the balls in these earrings are both decorative (adding dimensionality to the filigree) and supportive (adding

strength to the top joint where the piece connects to the earring hook).

Place the two 4mm balls at the top joints where the teardrops meet the lima beans. Add four of the 2–3mm balls over the other teardrop joints and the last two below the bottom lima [8]. You will have to add solder to the bottom two balls, but you may be able to use the existing solder in the teardrop joints to solder the other balls; if not, add solder as necessary. Pickle and rinse. Check to make sure that the balls are securely attached before you begin the polishing process.

Burnish the pieces, polish them, and add the earring hooks. *Voilà*—long, stylish earrings!

Variations

If you wish, replace the bottom balls with another set of parallel-end teardrops. After polishing, add dangles to the two teardrops on the sides and the one on the bottom.

Genie's Bottle Pendant

This charming pendant introduces adding a cabochon setting to your filigree work.

This is one of my earliest pendant designs that incorporates a gemstone. It uses primarily the witch's hat and variations of the witch's hat, as well as a teardrop, balls, and a cabochon (cab) setting. You can also use other types of settings. This will be the first design where you have to make non-standard filigree units. While this design is set up as a pendant, it also makes a nice earring design. Consider making a set.

YOU WILL NEED

- standard 1½-in. (3.8cm) witch's hat
- 1½-in. length of filigree wire
- 6cm length of filigree wire
- 1cm teardrop (overlapped)
- **3** silver balls: one 3–4mm, 2 2–3mm
- 10 x 12mm cabochon and setting
- 5–6mm jump ring

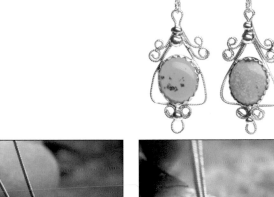

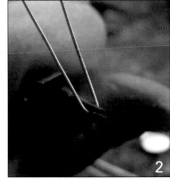

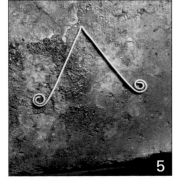

Being Flexible

Being flexible is what filigree is all about! You can use standard shapes or create new ones to fit the design. In this design, you will do a little of both.

1 Cut four lengths of filigree wire: two measuring 1½ in. (3.8cm), one measuring 6cm, and one measuring 1cm. Place the cab setting nearby **[1]**.

2–6 Begin this design by taking a 6cm length of filigree wire and bending it in two **[2]**, crimping the center **[3]**, and making a longer-than-usual witch's hat **[4]**. Make tight curls about 1½ times around **[5]**. When finished, place the cab setting inside the witch's hat **[6]**.

7 Put solder on the points where the setting and wire touch **[7]**. Because it's not a flat, horizontal surface, you will either need to place it alongside the wire or use the solder pick (see p. 53 for detailed instructions) to lift and move the solder where it needs to go. Solder, pickle, and rinse. When you solder these two pieces together, remember that the setting, being more massive, requires more heat to reach the same temperature as the wire. This means two

things: First, solder will flow to the warmer metal, so the solder won't attach to the setting until it's as warm as the wire. Second, because it takes more time to heat the setting, you should focus your heat on it first, and then on the wire, or you will end up melting your wire before the setting gets warm enough. One other tip to remember: Solder will flow toward the heat source. If your solder melts but doesn't flow toward the joint, you can often "tease" it to go over in the right direction by redirecting your flame from the direction you wish the solder to flow.

8–10 Now comes your first variation. Using your roundnose pliers, bend the ends of the witch's hat inward so that the spirals meet in the middle, under the cab setting [8]. Do this as symmetrically as possible. Make sure the spirals touch the base of the cab setting and each other. You will need to add solder by the base of the setting and between the two spirals [9]. Flux, solder [10], pickle, and rinse. Remember to heat the setting first, then focus on the wires. If the solder doesn't flow correctly, use the solder pick to guide it toward the joint.

11 After soldering the spirals together, place the teardrop between them. Add solder, and solder this piece in place [11].

12–14 Make a 1½-in. (3.8cm) witch's hat and fit it to the top point of your piece [12–14]. Flux and solder. Once the solder begins to flow, use your flame to draw it up and down the length of the witch's hat by moving the flame back and forth along the two legs of the piece. The solder will flow toward the flame and the joint between the two surfaces will look neater.

15–18 Next, we will be doing a variation on the witch's hat where, instead of adding a separate teardrop as we did in the star, we build it into the filigree unit. Begin with the usual 1½-in. strip of filigree wire, but when you bend it in half, do not crimp it in the middle. Instead, wrap it around your roundnose pliers [15]. Using your flatnose pliers, grip the two loose ends of the wire longways in the jaws of the flat pliers up to the base of the roundnose pliers [16]. When you are finished, you should end up with two parallel wires with a loop

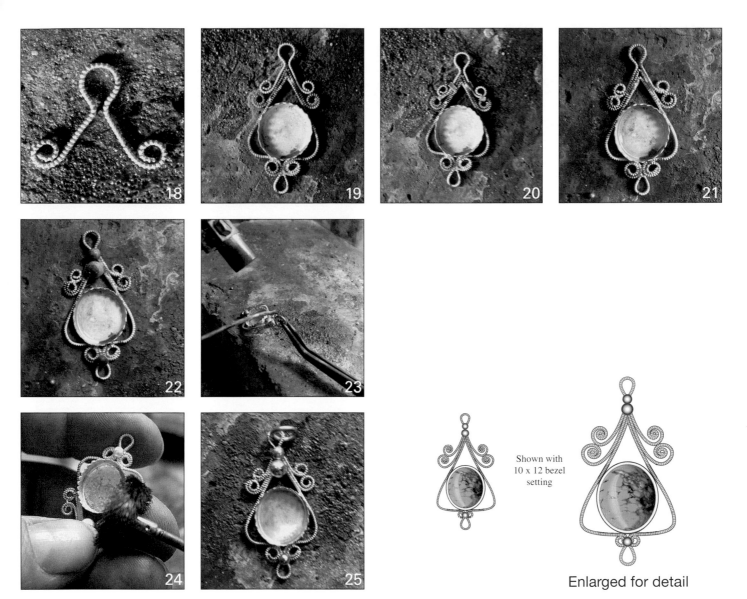

Shown with
10 x 12 bezel
setting

Enlarged for detail

at the end **[17]**. Use your roundnose pliers to bend out the two legs and make the typical loops of the witch's hat **[18]**. Your final piece should look like a shorter-than-usual witch's hat with a loop at the top.

19–21 Adjust the spirals and legs of the hat to fit on the top of your filigree piece so that the spirals of the first witch's hat and the second touch and the legs of the hats are flush together **[19]**. Flux and add solder along the legs and between the spirals **[20]**. Solder and pickle **[21]**.

22 Next, add silver balls, both for decoration and to cover multiple solder joints. Place a smaller ball where the three pieces meet at the bottom, and then place another smaller ball and a medium ball at the top of the triangular area above the cab setting. Put the smaller ball on the top so the balls follow the shape of the triangle **[22]**. Compare the piece to the illustrations above to make sure that all of the elements are in the right place. The silver balls here cover the multiple solder joints at the top, which are not really that pretty if exposed. You probably have enough solder

in these joints to attach the balls without adding extra, but add more if necessary. Flux, solder, pickle, and rinse.

23–25 Attach a jump ring to the top teardrop, and burnish and polish the piece **[23–25]**. When you are finished polishing the piece, place a drop of epoxy or cyanoacrylate glue (optional) in the setting. Place the cab in the setting and use a prong pusher or burnisher to press the edges of the setting over the cab, securing it in place.

The Four-leaf Clover

Use thicker wire to create a frame for traditional filigree shapes.

In this project, the use of a framework around the filigree is introduced. For most pieces, I use 18-gauge square wire for my frameworks. I occasionally use 16-gauge wire for larger pieces to create added strength. (Remember that with wire gauges, the smaller the number, the thicker and therefore the stronger the wire.) If you don't like the profile of square wire, another framework option is to use a thicker half-round wire for a framework with the flat side facing inward; 16-gauge works best. Using half-round wire adds a nice shape to the outside of the framework.

YOU WILL NEED
- **4** 1½-in. (3.8cm) matching limas
- **4** 1cm teardrops
- 3-in. (7.6cm) length of 18-gauge square wire
- ½-in. (1.3cm) length of 18-gauge square wire
- **4** 2–3mm silver balls
- **2** 4–5mm balls
- 5mm jump ring

Regardless of which profile wire you use, there are two basic purposes for the framework. One, naturally, is to provide strength and structural stability. The second is to add contrast between the highly polished framework and the patterned filigree wire.

You've Been Framed!
Frameworks can be closed or open. In this pendant, we will use a closed framework with filigree only on the inside. Once you gain more experience at filigree work and begin designing your own pieces, you can put filigree on the outside as well as the inside to make more complicated designs.

1–3 Your first step is to file flat the ends of a 3-in. (7.6cm) length of square wire. File the two ends so that they are flush when they meet. Then bend the wire into a circle **[1]**. If it's not exactly a circle at this point, that's okay. It will be easier to perfect the shape after it is soldered.

As with jump rings, make the two newly filed ends touch **[2]**. Flux the piece, place a solder chip on it, and solder, pickle, and rinse.

At this point, if you want to make your ring rounder, you can adjust it using your fingers and pliers. Or, if you have a ring mandrel, place the circle on the mandrel and use a rubber or nylon hammer to shape it to the roundness of the mandrel **[3]**.

4–5 The next step is to add a bail, which is the loop through which you will put a jump ring from which to suspend the pendant on a chain. In the previous projects, you made this loop with a piece of filigree wire. This wire was fine for such lightweight pieces, but when you add a heavier framework, you also increase the weight and therefore the drag on the bail. So for heavier pieces, I recommend using either more 18-gauge square wire or 18- or 16-gauge half-

round wire (flat side in) to make the bail. If you use a wire thicker than your framework, remember to taper it down to the same thickness where it connects to the framework.

For this piece, cut approximately ⅓ in. (1cm) of 18-gauge square wire. Make a U shape with the wire. Lay the circle framework down on your soldering area and place the U shape with the open end in toward the circle. Position this at the point where the circle was soldered together **[4]**. Check for fit; if need be, file the ends

of the U shape so they rest flush against the framework. Although these joints will be covered with a silver ball, they need to be well made to withstand wear. Flux, solder, pickle, and rinse **[5]**.

6–10 Now we begin adding filigree. Take four standard 1½-in. (3.8cm) lima beans and place them at the top, bottom, and sides of the framework, with the spiral ends facing toward the center. Don't worry about making a perfect fit; we will compensate with teardrops and silver balls.

For now, just make sure that the pieces are set up at the right points. Also, don't worry if the lima beans don't meet in the middle. If they overlap, compensate by adjusting the spirals to make the limas smaller.

Drip flux and place a solder chip on each joint where the lima beans touch the framework **[6]**, but do *not* add solder to the spirals on the limas just yet. Solder **[7]**, pickle, and rinse. If the symmetry of your piece is off, now is the time to correct it while the limas remain open. Make any

adjustments by curling the spirals in or out. Add solder chips to the spirals and solder, pickle, and rinse.

Place an overlapped teardrop in each corner between the lima beans, with the curves facing toward the center **[8]**. If the standard ⅓ in. (1cm) size is too large, cut something a little smaller and try again, but make sure all four teardrops are the same size. You will need to place solder on both sides of the teardrops to make sure they attach to each lima bean **[9]**. Don't worry if it seems like you're using too

much solder. It will be used up when you add the balls, so solder away! Your piece should now look similar to the one shown in **[10]**.

11–12 Select four small balls of approximately equal size to cover the points where the teardrops and limas meet. Lay them out on those spots. Choose a ball large enough to cover the opening in the center and to overlap onto the ends of the teardrops.

Place a large chip of solder in the middle of the piece, and then position the central ball. The solder chip should melt and solder the ball into place from underneath. Next, place another large ball at the junction between the bail and the framework to cover the solder joints at the top of the piece. (This ball is both cosmetic and structural, adding needed strength to this connection.)

The layout of your balls should be similar to the

layout shown in **[11]**. Add extra solder to the other balls if needed. Solder, pickle, and rinse **[12]**. Check to make sure the balls are securely soldered; if not, resolder as necessary.

Finally, burnish and polish the entire piece. Add your jump ring and chain, and your pendant is done!

Variations
As an alternative, you could replace the center ball with a small round

setting and gemstone. A cab setting could sit in between or across the ends of the teardrops **[figure 1]** , or a faceted stone setting could sit in between the teardrops **[figure 2]**.

Actual size

Enlarged for detail

FIGURE 1

FIGURE 2

The Heart Pendant

Set a faceted gemstone in the center of this heart pendant.

In this project, you'll make a heart-shaped pendant using square wire for the framework and several of the heart-shaped filigree shapes you practiced making earlier (or make new ones now). You'll also add a faceted gemstone for ornamentation.

YOU WILL NEED

- 3 in. (7.6cm) 18-gauge square wire
- about ⅜ in. (1cm) 18-gauge square wire
- filigree wire: 3½-in. (8.9cm), 2⅜-in. (6cm), and 1½-in. (3.8cm) lengths
- gemstone and setting (maximum size 6mm round or 6 x 4mm oval or pearl)
- 6–7mm jump ring
- 3 3–4mm silver balls

Setting faceted stones is a much more complicated matter than setting simple flat-back cabochons, so I will not go into depth on it here. Instead, I recommend buying easy-mount, pre-notched, or snap-set solderable settings for projects that contain faceted gems. These three setting types are easy enough for most people to use without any formal training or special tools beyond pliers and needle files. See "Resources," page 112, for a list of suppliers.

Put Your Work in Your Heart . . .

I find I put my heart in my work, but here's a chance to put some work in your heart. Hearts are extremely popular, and the shape is especially adaptable to filigree work. This is a very basic design that's elevated by the addition of a faceted gemstone. Feel free to leave the stone off or, if you wish, substitute a cab setting.

1–3 First, cut a strip of square wire 3 in. (7.6cm) long. Mark the center of the strip (1½ in./

3.8cm) [1]. Take a triangular or similar needle file and notch the center about one-third of the way through the wire [2]. This will give you a sharper bend at the bottom of the square wire.

Bend the wire into a wide V shape [3]. When you begin to solder, you will end up soldering the notch in the bottom, so it won't be a weak spot.

4–5 Your next step is to curl the two ends into partial spirals or gentle curves. Carefully bend one end toward the middle. Then

bend the other, trying to keep the two curves as equal as possible. Continue to adjust them until they meet in the middle. File the two ends so that they are flush against each other for soldering.

Place a chip of solder where the wires meet at the center top of the heart and another chip at the bottom point [4]. Solder; your heart framework should be similar to the one shown in [5]. Manipulate the framework with your fingers and roundnose pliers if the halves of the heart aren't quite symmetrical.

6–14 Next, create an assortment of heart shapes **[6-8]**. The first heart should be made from a 3½-in. (8.9cm) strip of filigree wire. Bend in half and curl. The curls on the ends should be minimal. Test-fit the heart by placing it in the framework; it should sit flush on the inside, with the loops positioned just below the V at the top of the heart **[9]**. Place several solder chips, evenly spaced, around the heart frame so that when they melt, the solder will flow in and fill the space between the framework and the first heart **[10]**. Use the flame to draw the molten solder around the frame by moving the torch back and forth or around the frame. Solder, pickle, and rinse.

Make another, smaller heart from a 2⅜-in. (6cm) length of filigree wire **[11]**. Keep the sides of this heart straighter than the framework, so that when placed into the larger heart it touches only the base, one place on either side, and the curls of the first heart. For a proper fit, you will need to spread the two lobes of the heart apart. You may have to adjust the spirals in or out to make it fit tightly. Use the tension in the wire to hold it in place. Solder, pickle, and rinse **[12]**.

Make the last heart from a 1½-in. (3.8cm) length of wire **[13]**. This time, leave the heart in a closed position and fit it into the middle of the heart framework so it only touches the base and curls of the last heart added. Adjust the curls in or out to make it fit tightly. If necessary, adjust the curls from the second

filigree heart in or out. Make sure the whole thing is as symmetrical as possible. Add solder chips **[14]** and solder, pickle and rinse.

15 Take a ⅜-in. (1cm) piece of square wire and bend it into an overlapped teardrop. Clip and then file the ends so the tips fit where they meet and create a point. Place a large chip of solder over this new joint **[15]** and solder.

16 Next, add a setting for the faceted gemstone. You can use up to a 5 or 6mm setting with this piece (any larger and the setting won't fit). Choose a round or oval setting, or even a pear-shaped setting but invert it so the point faces down. The stone in this example is a 5mm round set in a snap-set

setting. You will be soldering the setting to the spirals in the middle of the heart. If you use a larger setting that spans down and touches other places in the heart, solder there as well.

There are two ways of attaching the setting. The first is to put the setting in place and lay out solder chips as usual **[16]**. The other way is to melt solder onto the sides of the spirals before placing the setting. Pickle and rinse. Then, place the setting, flux, and remelt the solder that was just placed. Use your solder pick to nudge the setting into place or to straighten its position if it shifts.

Here's another soldering tip: As we discussed in the chapter on tools (p. 23), solder comes in different melting temperatures: hard,

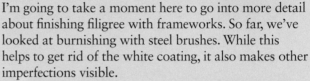

FINISHING PIECES WITH FRAMEWORKS

I'm going to take a moment here to go into more detail about finishing filigree with frameworks. So far, we've looked at burnishing with steel brushes. While this helps to get rid of the white coating, it also makes other imperfections visible.

Cratex wheels, discussed in "Tools and Supplies," p. 23, can be used to clean up frameworks made of square wire. Be sure to keep the flexible shaft moving to keep the finish even. If you stay in one place too long, you risk digging a deeper groove in the silver.

Exercise caution when using a Cratex wheel around a set stone; it is abrasive enough to damage the polished surface on most gems. If you must use a Cratex wheel on bezel settings, for example, take it slow and controlled. Don't touch the set stone, or you will have to find a way to repolish it.

medium, easy, and sometimes extra-easy. When adding a setting to a piece, I suggest going down a step in solder to avoid melting the prongs. (Settings can range from a few cents to several dollars each, and it's no fun ruining one) For example, if you are using medium solder for the general piece, drop to easy to attach the setting. If you are proficient in soldering, this isn't necessary, but if you are new to soldering, go down a step. You'll apply less heat to the setting and thus avoid melting it. Another solder option for settings is to use paste solder, which you can squeeze into the area between the filigree and the setting.

17–19 Next, add balls where the bail meets the heart, in

the open area between the first and third filigree heart, and at the bottom where all the hearts meet **[17–18]**. Solder, pickle, and rinse. Afterward, add the jump ring **[19]** and set the stone. (Before setting the stone, make sure that the silver balls are securely attached. If you need to resolder them, do so before setting the stone; otherwise, the stone could be damaged during the soldering process.)

20–21 Buff and polish the piece **[20–21 and sidebar]**.

Actual Size

Enlarged for detail

Raindrop Pendant

Choose your favorite setting and stone for the focal point of this pendant.

This project introduces individual spirals as well as filigree outside of a framework. It's a simple yet elegant pendant to showcase a gemstone. The best part of this design is that it's so open, which means it can embrace a gemstone of almost any size, shape, or type, and it can be used with either a cab or prong setting. Choose a stone that's particularly attractive to you. If you prefer, you can simplify this project by using the upper loop to hang a beaded dangle.

YOU WILL NEED
- **10+** spirals (using 1³⁄₁₆-in. [3cm] strips)
- **5** teardrops (using ³⁄₈-in. [1cm] strips)
- teardrop (using ⁵⁄₈-in. [1.5cm] strip)
- 2³⁄₄ in. (7cm) 18-gauge square wire
- ³⁄₈ in. (1cm) 18-gauge square wire
- **9** silver balls (**2** 3–5mm and **7** 2–3mm)
- stone and setting of your choice
- 6–7mm jump ring

A Drop in the Filigree Bucket . . .

As I'm sure you are starting to understand, there are infinite numbers of variations and patterns of filigree, and the few we've done so far in this book are just a (rain)drop in the proverbial bucket.

1–4 Begin by taking a 2³⁄₄-in. (7cm) length of square wire and shaping it into a large teardrop **[1]**. (For clarity,

I'll now refer to this large teardrop as a raindrop.) File the inside of the two wires so that they meet flush against each other and solder the joint. File the top tip of the raindrop flat **[2]**. Make a small teardrop from the ³⁄₈-in. (1cm) square wire, filing it so the ends meet neatly in the center. File the tip flat and place it against the raindrop point to point. Add a large solder chip **[3]** and solder the joint **[4]**. Pickle and rinse. You may

want to go over the wire with a file or Cratex wheel to smooth out any imperfections, which will shorten the time you spend finishing at the end. Or, if you have a rolling mill, you can run the frame through the flat rollers at a very slightly reduced thickness, evening out the frame. Don't worry about the area where the raindrop and the teardrop meet; this will be covered by a silver ball, and any excess solder can be used to attach the ball.

5–10 Using 1³⁄₁₆-in. (3cm) strips of filigree wire, make a handful of single spirals similar to those shown in **[5]**. You will need 10 for the project, but it is a good idea to make extras so you can find matching spirals and have replacements in case you melt one or two in the soldering process. Make a single spiral, and then compare each successive spiral to that one. They won't be identical, but if

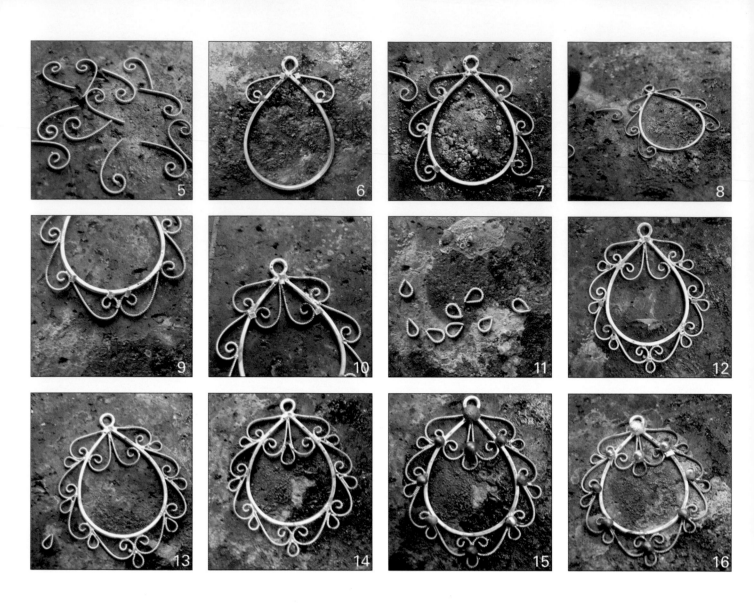

they are close, you can manage to make the piece as symmetrical as possible.

Divide the spirals into matching pairs. You can make small adjustments as you go before soldering each pair into place. Begin by taking one pair and laying the tails of each spiral into the corners created by the raindrop and teardrop of the framework. Make sure the spirals are in the same position on each side of the frame and that they are snug against the framework **[6]**. Flux, solder, pickle, and rinse.

When you have finished the first pair, try adding the next two matching pairs, for a total of four pieces to solder at one time **[7]**. If you

don't feel comfortable doing two pairs, take them one pair at a time. (Don't add the last two spirals at the bottom at the same time as you add these pairs. The bottom spirals may need to be adjusted, depending on the lengths of the other spirals.) Solder **[8]**, pickle, and rinse.

Next, add the bottom spirals **[9]**. Unless you are very lucky, you will have to adjust them either in or out. Make sure that the spirals are symmetrical and meet in the middle of the pendant. Solder the spirals.

Place the remaining two spirals inside the top of the framework, with the spirals facing out toward the framework **[10]**. Solder as usual.

11–14 Make seven overlapping teardrops using ³⁄₈-in. (1cm) strips **[11]**. Divide six of them into matching pairs; if one of the seven is slightly larger or smaller, use that one for the bottom point of the piece. Place the teardrops where each spiral meets the next on the outside of the framework **[12]** and solder, pickle, and rinse. Don't worry if gaps or extra solder are visible **[13]**; fix these problems on the next round of soldering, or use the solder pick to reposition teardrops and place solder on any unfinished joints.

Make a larger teardrop using a ⁵⁄₈-in. (1.5cm) strip. Position it between the two

spirals on the inside of the framework **[14]**, but save soldering it for the next step.

15–17 Select seven small (2–3mm) balls to go over the teardrops outside the framework. Unless your balls are identical, pair them up before laying them out on the joints, using the seventh for the bottom teardrop. Add solder if necessary.

Next, choose two more balls (3–5mm in size). Place the larger ball at the joint between the teardrop and the raindrop, and place the smaller ball on the teardrop inside the framework **[15]**. (Remember, this teardrop hasn't been soldered into

17

18

19

20

21

22

23

FIGURE 1

placc yet; the solder chip placed here should be sufficient for both the teardrop and the ball.) Solder **[16–17]**, using the solder pick to keep the balls in their places. Pickle and rinse.

18 Now that the framework and the filigree are done, it's time to add the setting. I used a 14 x 12mm stone with a prong setting, but you can use the stone and setting of your choice.

Place your setting at the midpoint of the lower part of your framework. You have two options here, as mentioned in Project 6 (p. 66): Either place the solder next to the prongs **[18]**, or melt solder onto the inside of the framework, place the setting against the already melted solder, and remelt it. With the second option, the solder will flow between the setting and the framework. If the solder is placed next to the setting, it can flow into the filigree below the setting or become a lump on the framework. If this happens, carefully take your solder pick and

push the semi-molten solder toward the setting. The solder pick also can be used to smooth the aforementioned "lumps" of solder if caught while still semi-molten.

19–20 Add a jump ring through the bail using your bent locking tweezers **[19]**, solder the jump ring closed **[20]**, and you're finished soldering.

21–23 Burnish and polish the piece. Since this piece is somewhat more complex than those in previous projects, I want to go over the importance of burnishing with a steel brush **[21–23]**. The steel brush gets into small areas that are hard to polish with the larger brushes on a polishing motor. Burnishing is also useful for getting around the base of silver balls, around settings, and in areas where filigree meets a framework. The only other way to get into these nooks and crannies is to tumble polish.

Actual size

If you don't use the steel brush on a complex piece, you run the risk of having leftover white, matte areas around the balls and in tight spaces. These areas don't look particularly professional when the rest of a piece has a high polish.

After polishing, set the stone. Do any touch-up polishing around the setting, such as removing marks from your pliers or filing down an excess prong.

Variations
As mentioned earlier, this design has a lot of flexibility. Sometimes I like to vary it by using a cab setting, or by suspending pearl dangles

FIGURE 2

from the teardrops, as shown in **figures 1** and **2**. It can also be used to showcase lampworked beads.

The Little Butterfly

Arrange spirals and limas into a butterfly shape to make this pendant.

A charming pendant for a little girl, this piece has a frame similar to the one in the previous project. However, this pendant also features a central bar for added support. Silver balls are also used here, but in a slightly different way.

YOU WILL NEED
- 2½ in. (6.4cm) 18-gauge square wire
- about ⅜ in. (1cm) 18-gauge square wire
- about ⅝ in. (1.5cm) 18-gauge square wire
- **3** strips of filigree wire, 1½ in. (3.8cm) each
- **7** silver balls (**6** 2–3mm and **1** 4mm)
- 3–4mm stone and setting
- 6mm jump ring

On the Wings of a Butterfly . . .

Fine filigree can be made to resemble the veins in a butterfly's wings. In this case, the filigree is the butterfly's wings and antennae. Although only a few shapes are used in this piece, even minimal amounts of filigree can make a very striking pendant.

1–3 Start with a 2½-in. (6.4cm) piece of square wire, and make and solder a slightly-wider-than-usual teardrop shape **[1]**. Next, take the ⅝-in. (1.5cm) strip of square wire and give it a gentle curve. File the ends of this wire to fit snugly against the inner sides of the teardrop. Place it inside the teardrop **[2]**. Take the ⅜-in. (1cm) piece of square wire and make a teardrop. This time, file the ends of the drop to fit on the point of the larger teardrop. If you prefer, you can do as you did in Project 7 (p. 70) and file both points flat. Fit the teardrop into place, and solder, pickle, and rinse **[3]**.

4–11 Bend two of the 1½-in. (4cm) strips of filigree wire into L shapes **[4]**. Make sure you bend both of them at the same point along the wire so that your final two pieces will be symmetrical. These will be the wings of the butterfly.

Maintain the right angle and, one at a time, bend each end of the wire into a spiral until the spirals meet **[5–6]**. The upper spiral should sit farther out than the lower spiral **[7]**. Repeat with the other wire. Place them next to each other **[8]** and adjust the spirals until they look like butterfly wings. Place the spirals in the framework but leave a space between them **[9]**; solder the pieces into place.

Next, make a witch's hat **[10]**. This will be the antennae. You will have to adjust the legs to fit into the upper triangle of the pendant **[11]**; solder into place.

12–16 Now, add the setting. This project is an example of placing the solder first, before you melt it. Place a solder chip inside the frame **[12]**, add flux, and melt the solder, attaching it to the center support. Pickle, rinse, flux, and *then* place the setting and remelt the solder to attach the setting **[13]**. You may need your solder pick to adjust the position of the setting or to push it into the solder. A 3–4mm prong setting and 4mm stone were used in this project as the head of the butterfly, but you can also use a cab setting if you prefer.

Make the butterfly's body from three silver balls. You'll need to find three balls of decreasing size, starting with the first ball being slightly smaller than the butterfly's head (the set stone) **[14]**. This will make a tapered body in the space between the two wings and under the head or setting. The balls should fit the area as tightly as possible. Add solder around the balls and solder **[15]**, pickle, and rinse.

After completing the body, add a couple more decorative/supporting balls: one large one at the top and three smaller ones across the middle (two where the crossbar meets the frame and one between the head and antennae) **[16]**.

Add a jump ring, polish the piece, and set the stone, and your pendant is finished.

Actual size

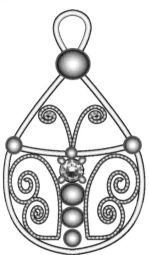

Enlarged for detail

The Lupin

This freeform filigree pendant is the perfect way to showcase an asymmetrical stone.

Art often imitates nature, and this design is no exception. I call this design "the lupin" because its billowy top reminds me of the lupin flower, which grows wild in Norway and other parts of the world, including North America. Domesticated cultivars often flourish in the typical English cottage garden. The lupin design is also one I use when I have an asymmetrical stone, as it is extremely adaptable. The pattern naturally changes from stone to stone, so in this project, I will not specify lengths of filigree wire—you get to use your own judgment.

YOU WILL NEED
- filigree wire
- aproximately 1½-2 in. (3.8-5cm) 18-gauge square wire
- fine bezel wire or sterling strip wire
- thin sterling sheet for backing
- asymmetrical cabochon
- 8 2–5mm silver balls
- accent stone and prong setting (optional)

Watch how this design is put together, but don't try to follow the specific design. Instead, play off the shape of your irregular stone and develop a feel for the general flow of the lupin design.

In this project I also will give a brief overview on how to make a setting for an irregular cab and how to set such a stone.

Let Your Creativity Blossom!
With this project, not only will the pendant blossom as you build it, but your creativity and intuition will blossom as well. You will develop the individual spirals and the exact pattern arrangements, taking your cue from the irregular stone you choose. However, there are some basic steps you should follow when making this kind of design, which works well for either pendants (simply add a bail and chain) or brooches (add a pin back to the back of the stone setting).

In a way, asymmetrical pendants are easier than symmetrical pieces because you don't have to worry about making matching units. However, they are also more difficult because even an asymmetrical design must have balance and a sense of flow—something that is almost inherent in a symmetrical design. An asymmetrical design does not mean a random or haphazard design. It must be balanced visually and physically, so the piece hangs correctly as well as being visually appealing.

In some ways, the lupin design reminds me of fractals, a mathematical phenomenon. Fractals are mathematical equations that produce small patterns on a seemingly random level, but with an overall appearance that shows a pattern or structure on a larger level. On one level, you just place spirals along a central framework wire, but the overall appearance should be balanced and present a coherent structure and appearance.

I use the lupin design a lot with either asymmetrical stone cabochons or dichroic glass cabs, which are often irregular in shape. I have also used this pattern in an elongated form I call a "comet," with a symmetrical gemstone as the head and an asymmetrical tail trailing off. The comet makes an especially nice brooch. The photo above shows an assortment of lupins using asymmetrical and symmetrical stones.

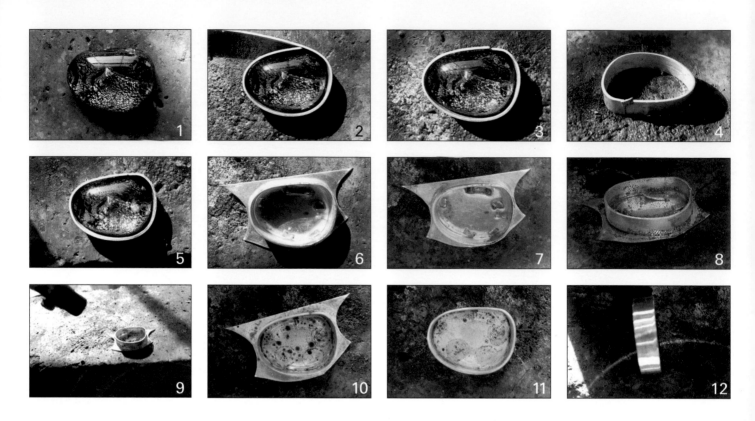

Create a Bezel Setting

1–16 First, select a good-sized asymmetrical stone to use for the project; the one I used is a dichroic glass cabochon, roughly 20 x 15mm **[1]**. Next, make a bezel for the stone. You can use either fine bezel wire, which is very soft and easy to bend (making it easier to form the setting), or you can use sterling-silver strip wire. The latter requires more pressure to bend it over the stone when you set it.

Bend whichever wire you choose around the stone and mark where it overlaps **[2]**. Clip the wire at this point and file both ends of the bezel so the two ends will fit snugly against each other. Check the fit around the stone and make any adjustments needed **[3]**. Remove the stone and prepare to solder. Flux the bezel and place a chip of solder at the top of the joint. Remember to warm the entire bezel before concentrating the

flame on the joint. The solder should flow into the joint. If it doesn't, or if it falls off before you can get the solder to flow, use the solder pick to transport solder where you need it. Solder **[4]**, pickle, and rinse.

After soldering, test fit the stone into the bezel **[5]**. At this point, it can be helpful to roll the setting with the stone in it along a hard surface. This will give you a more exact fit around the stone.

Next, make a backing for the stone. Take a piece of thin silver sheet a little larger than what you will need (use either a scrap piece or cut one roughly to fit). Make sure the bottom edge of your bezel is as even as possible; file it if necessary. Place the bezel on the silver sheet. Flux the setting and place chips of solder along the inside of the bezel **[6]**.

Here's a soldering tip for you: Apply your flux, then heat slightly—just enough to evaporate the water in the flux without burning off the

flux itself—and then place the solder. Otherwise, the boiling flux tends to move the solder chips away from the sides and into the middle of the setting.

Warm the entire piece by moving the torch in a circular motion over the setting. When the solder begins to melt, use your flame to draw it toward the nearest side and into the gap between the bezel and the sheet **[7]**. While the solder is molten, drag the flame around the setting and make the solder fill in the gap around the entire setting **[8–10]**.

After the bezel is soldered to its backing, you need to remove the excess silver sheet from the setting **[11]**. You can choose whichever method you feel most comfortable doing. The "proper" way to do it is by sawing away the excess with a jeweler's saw, but personally I'm not patient enough with the saw for this approach—and I tend to

break a lot of blades in my impatience. Instead, I use metal shears. (Use these with care, as they can distort the setting if the blades twist.) Once you remove the excess sheet, clean up the setting's edge by filing away the last of the excess sheet, either manually with a hand file or mechanically with a flexible shaft tool such as a Dremel **[12–16]**.

Lay a piece of dental floss across the bezel setting. Add your cabochon and check its fit again to make sure the bezel walls weren't damaged during the cleanup stage. If your stone fits really tightly, you'll be glad of the dental floss—just pull on both ends of it to pop the stone back out. Set the stone aside until needed at the end.

Add the Wire Framework

17–21 Cut a piece of 18-gauge square wire between 1½ and 2 in. (3.8–5cm) in length **[17]**. Use your fingers to give

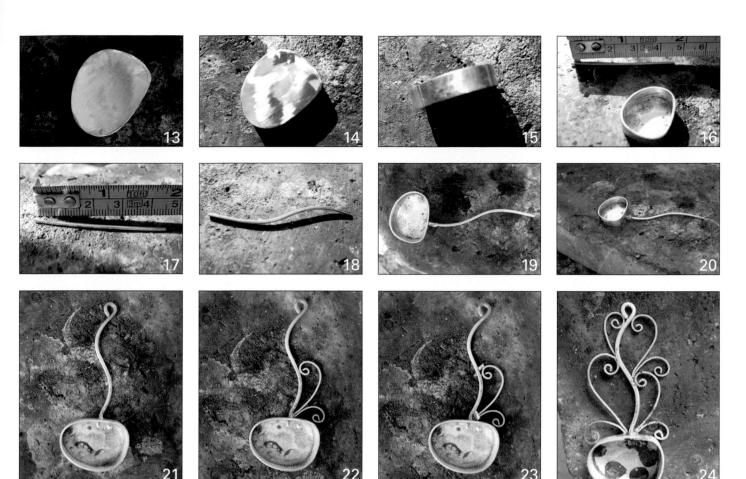

it a wavy appearance [18]. File the end smooth and solder the wire to the setting [19]; it doesn't have to be in the dead center of the setting. Use your intuition instead, making sure that the curved wire and setting are visually balanced. You can make adjustments to the curve after you solder it, but you need to find a basic balance in that first piece of wire, so spend your time deciding where to add it.

In pieces with large cab settings, you will find that the larger the setting, the harder it may be to get the solder to flow between the setting and the framework (and the same holds true when adding filigree to the setting). The reason for this is that it takes more heat to warm up the setting than it does the surrounding wire. Thus, make sure you heat

FIGURE 1

the setting first, then the framework or filigree you wish to attach. Use your solder pick if necessary, either to add more solder or to coax the solder into the gap between the setting and the framework or filigree.

Set the piece flat on your work surface [20] and make sure the framework is level with the surface; now is the time to adjust it if it is not. Use your roundnose pliers to make a teardrop-shaped bail at the end of the square wire [21].

Add Filigree

22–30 Now comes the first filigree in this piece. I usually add a double spiral, where the spirals are uneven and facing away from each other (kind of a distorted witch's hat) [22 and **figure 1**]. One spiral should attach to the framework, and the other should attach to the bezel. Add solder as you work [23]. (Sometimes, it's easier to solder one of the spirals to the center point, and then go back and reposition the other spiral before soldering.)

I usually use two to four of these units as the basic framework for this design [24]. These filigree units make the basic lupin structure of the pendant. Sizes will vary, and you can place spirals along the central framework. I find that placing spirals above,

below, or on the bend in the wire creates a natural and balanced look. Near the top of the pendant, you may want to use a single spiral instead of a double in order to keep the lupin-like appearance. You'll also want to tuck in single spirals in any areas that seem too airy [25–26].

Solder these pieces into place to create the general structure of the piece [27]. Be careful not to melt the inner loops where the base of the filigree connects to the setting. If any of the loops melt, you can either replace the piece or compensate by placing a silver ball over that loop.

Once you have this structure in place, fill in the gaps in the filigree [28]. You cannot leave the piece as open as it is in [24]; the fine wires need support.

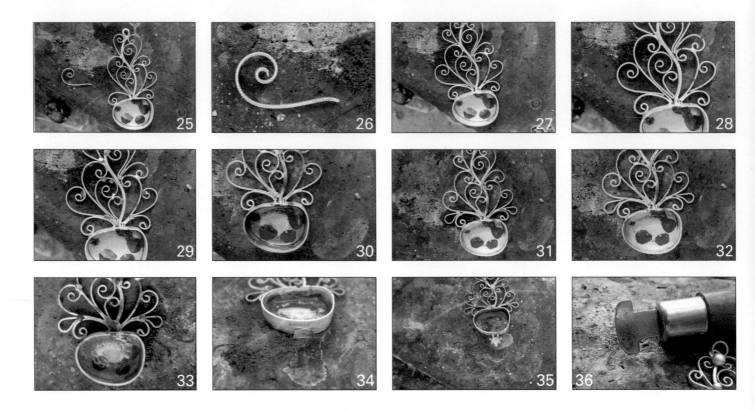

Solder the larger pieces in place first, so you can take smaller, internal spirals and put them into open areas, where the tension in the wire will help keep them in place. In this piece, I soldered quite a few pieces at one time, but you can break down the process as much as you need to and add pieces one or two at a time.

It's not necessary to fill every spiral with another. Sometimes, leaving a spiral open and adding a piece on the outside for support can be more attractive than trying to make sure all the gaps are filled.

Another thing to consider when using single and double spirals is making them fit wherever you want to place them. Sometimes, you need to bend the end of the curl in the opposite direction in order to make it fit deeper into an opening. You can also crimp the end of a wire, as you do when bending a wire in two. Use the base of the jaws of your roundnose pliers to squeeze the end of the wire into a thinner point so that it can get down into the juncture created by two spirals meeting. With practice, you can even use varying degrees of pressure to taper the end of the wire with this technique. (I prefer this to filing the end of the wire. Small pieces of wire are hard to file with any degree of control, and you can end up filing more of your fingertips than the wire.)

Once you have laid out the pieces you want and are pleased with their arrangement, solder them. Remember to put solder on *all* the places where two wires touch each other **[29]**, and solder the pieces **[30]**. If they don't all solder successfully, either repeat the soldering process or use your solder pick to add solder as needed. Pickle and rinse when finished.

The next step is adding teardrops to finish off some of the remaining places where two spirals meet. You will have to decide which places need them and which do not. You also do not need to use the standard ⅜-in. (1cm) wire length used in previous projects. Sometimes you will need a larger drop for one place and a smaller drop for another. You may also find that you need to make a teardrop lopsided to maintain a general flow to the design. In this particular example, I only added them to the two lower spiral meeting-places in order to maintain the tapered look of the pendant **[31–32]**. If I had added teardrops to the upper joints, they would have had to be very small or they would have made the upper part of the pendant too broad.

Embellishing

33 The next step is adding the silver balls. Place balls over the triple joints where two spirals and a teardrop meet, as well as at the top and bottom of the wire framework down the middle. Beyond that, you will have to decide where they are needed, either to cover up ugly joints or to make the overall pattern of balls look balanced. Select the appropriate-size ball for the joint in question. For example, I used heavier balls along the main 18-gauge framework and smaller balls along the actual filigree **[33]**. Basically, if you have a place with several joints, your silver ball needs to cover all of the joints.

Assembly

34–35 In my example, I chose to add a faceted accent stone at the base of the dichroic glass cab. Melt solder a step down from what you've been using (from hard to medium, from medium to easy, and so on). Apply flux and the selected solder at the outside of the bezel along the bottom **[34]** and melt the solder. Position the prong setting and melt

37

38

39

40

41

42

43

the solder again to attach the two settings **[35]**.

This process may seem a bit cumbersome, but it's easier than trying to get the solder chip to sit and flow between the two settings. Having it melted onto the larger setting ensures that the solder will flow from the larger setting to the smaller. (Going from smaller to larger is more difficult because of the heat issues discussed earlier.)

Add a jump ring and solder it shut. After you have finished soldering, burnish and polish the filigree and the settings.

Set the Stones

36–42 At this point, you need to set the main stone.

Fine bezel wire is easiest to use if you want to just bend the bezel over onto the stone. To bend the wire over, use a prong pusher **[36]** to gently push the wire down onto the stone, smoothing as you go.

I used sterling-silver strip wire, which is thicker and stiffer than fine bezel wire. Before I could fold over the silver strip, I had to make adjustments so the strip would fold and lie correctly. I notched the setting so that the bezel could fold over without bulging **[37–38]**.

Usually, I notch the corners of a setting, but in this case I had to work around the second setting, so I made notches in the sides and in the spot where the second setting would be placed. Use a round needle file or a round flexible shaft bore (dental bores are good). Make the notches deep enough that the remaining strip can be bent over the curve of the cab in a natural fashion. Once it is notched, go over the setting with a Cratex wheel to smooth out some of the sharper edges, and then put your cab in place. If you find your setting is a little too big, glue your stone in place before setting it so that it remains in the center.

Now place the pendant where you can hold it securely. Use a bench pin if you have one. (A bench pin is a wooden support used for a wide variety of jewelry-making applications.) Brace the pendant with your non-dominant hand and take the prong pusher in your dominant hand **[39]**. Place the edge of the prong pusher against the strip/bezel and push it into place. Once a length of bezel is in place, rock the prong pusher from side to side, smoothing the bent-over bezel against the

cab. Once you have one segment in place, move on to the next. Go over the whole bezel a couple of times to make sure it sits flush and even against the cab **[40–42]**. **[43]** shows a bezel partly in place around the cabochon.

When you are finished, file away any marks with a needle file or Cratex wheel. (If you use the Cratex wheel, be very careful around your stone so the Cratex wheel does not damage the finish.)

Set the accent stone, and then do any touch-up polishing around the settings.

Actual size

Enlarged for detail

Swirl Ring

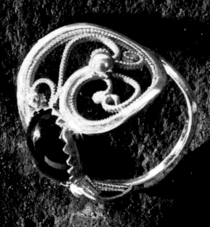

Bend a simple two-dimensional swirl into three dimensions to create a pinky ring.

In this project, we'll break from the two-dimensionality of previous projects and make a ring. This ring pattern is designed to fit a left-hand pinky or ring finger. If you wish to wear it on your right hand, reverse the design. Use the illustration on p. 87 as your guide to shaping the wire; after this form is made, you'll reshape the flat filigree into a ring.

YOU WILL NEED
- 4–5 in. (10-12.7cm) 18-gauge square wire
- 3-in. (7.6cm) strip filigree wire
- 2 1-in. (2.5cm) strips filigree wire
- 1½ in. (3.8cm) strip of filigree wire
- serrated cab setting
- 8 x 10mm cab
- 3 2–3mm silver balls

And Now, to "Ring" in Project 10!

The nice thing about filigree is that you can work flat in two dimensions and then bend the piece into three dimensions—in this case, a ring. The hard part, of course, is bending the ring into its final shape without distorting the cab setting.

1–6 Start with a piece of 18-gauge square wire 4–5 in. (10–12.7cm) long **[1]**. If you have small fingers, use the smaller measurement. For larger fingers, use the larger measurement. Any excess will be cut off after you bend the ring, so you needn't pay too much attention to length just yet.

Make a spiral **[2]** with the square wire. Then take a 3-in. (7.6cm) length of filigree wire and shape it into a similar curl that can fit inside the heavier curl, tight against the framework **[3]**.

Work the filigree spiral into the framework **[4]**. Fit it in as snugly as possible, but don't worry about getting it perfect on the first try. Instead, find one point to solder, which will hold it in place. Flux, solder, pickle,

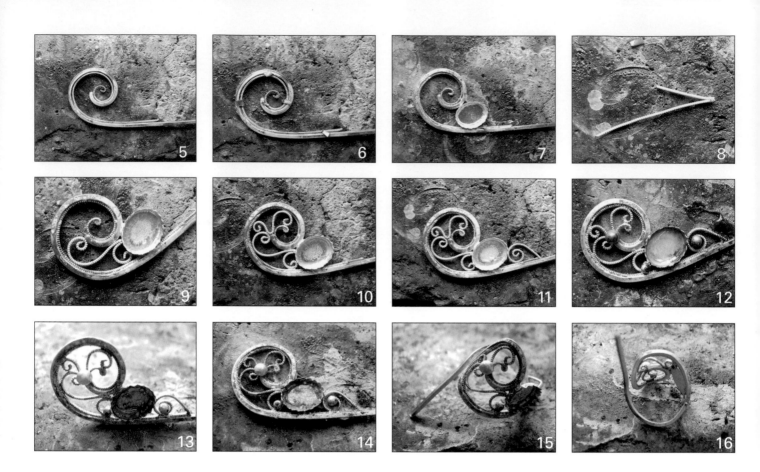

and rinse. Once you have soldered this point, the springiness of the filigree wire will disappear and it will be easier to push the wire into place and make it stay there. (Tip: When you are fitting one spiral inside another spiral, make the inside spiral larger than needed, and then push it into place **[5]**. This should help it fit securely.)

Once you have the filigree wire inside the framework where you want it, place solder along the length of the piece **[6]**. Flux, solder, pickle, and rinse. While soldering, remember to drag the flame back and forth along the wire, which will force the solder to flow back and forth and fill in the gaps. If you find that some points don't fill with solder, try adding more with the solder pick. If a gap is too big to fill, then after rinsing, use your pliers to gently squeeze the

filigree wire and the wall of the framework together and reheat. You may not need to add extra solder if there is enough from before. The solder should flow into the gap now.

7 Next, we're going to add a cab setting. You could also use a faceted setting, but for this example I used an 8 × 10mm serrated cab setting. Solder it between the spiral framework and the long side of the spiral. Make sure you have solder on both sides of the setting so that it attaches at both contact points. For best results, place the solder chips down along the sides of the framework, next to the setting **[7]**. Solder as usual.

8–11 Take a 1½-in. (3.8cm) piece of filigree wire and bend it into an L shape. Bend it all the way back onto itself and

use the base of the jaws of your pliers to pinch it at the bend **[8]**. Make the smaller of the spirals first, bending it outward. Then bend the larger spiral, also outward. You should be able to fit it into the framework **[9]**. The smaller curl should fit snugly up against the setting, and the larger should fit between the coils of the spiral framework. The filigree should resemble a wavelike pattern.

Now, take a 1-in. (2.5cm) strip of filigree wire and make a similar piece, without pinching the bend. Wedge this piece in the center of the spiral framework **[10]**. Flux, solder, pickle, and rinse.

Use another 1-in. (2.5cm) strip to make the last piece of filigree. Make a simple spiral and solder it in place on the other side of the setting, along the frame wire **[11]**. Position the spiral so that the tail of the spiral meets

the end of the filigree wire soldered to the main frame. Make sure you solder all three points where the spiral meets the setting and the framework.

12–13 Take three balls and place the largest over the end of the spiral's framework where several joints meet. Place the other two on the center loop of the two spirals closest to the setting **[12]**. You may not need extra solder on the first ball, but you will need it on the other two. Flux, solder, pickle, and rinse **[13]**.

14–25 Now comes the hardest part: bending this piece so that you can turn it into a ring. Use your fingers and/or pliers to begin bending the main swirl and the swirl behind the setting into a ring shape **[14–15]**. Be very

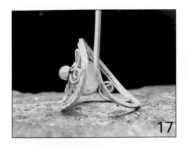

careful *not* to bend the setting or you will have a hard time setting your stone afterward.

Drag the tail of the framework around and twist it back toward the long part of the spiral **[16–17]**. Place the ring on a ring mandrel and position it at the approximate size you desire **[18–20]**. Use a rubber or nylon hammer to hammer on the filigree sections and the tail to shape it properly, but take care not to hit the cab setting. Use light taps with the hammer **[21–23]** to make small changes in the ring's shape, rather than trying to bludgeon the piece into shape with one blow.

Once you've reached the approximate size, cut off the excess tail. File the end of the wire so it will fit flush against the front part of the ring **[24]**, forming a V

shape. Add a chip of solder in the V shape where the tail meets the framework, or use your solder pick to place it. Flux, solder **[25]**, and pickle, keeping it in the pickle long enough to get rid of all the red and black oxidation. Rinse.

26–28 Test the inside of the ring for any snags that might scratch the wearer **[26]**. Follow the usual polishing routine of burnishing and

using Cratex wheels, then polishing on the polisher.

When you have finished polishing the piece, select an 8 x 10mm cab. Since rings suffer more abuse than other pieces of jewelry, add a little glue to your setting for security (a water-based, clear-drying epoxy is recommended). Place the stone and let the glue dry **[27]**. Roll your prong pusher over the serrated edges of the setting, pushing them in toward the ring. Because the

ring sits askew on the finger, it will fit best on your left pinky finger as we've made it today. As a pinky ring, the filigree wraps around the side of your finger with the stone on the top of your finger **[28]**.

Actual size

Enlarged for detail

Fan Dangle Necklace

Two main components—
a fan and a dangle—
make up this necklace.

Now it's time to take all of your newly-developed skills and put them together in one large, complex project. The individual parts are not difficult, but the final result will be something special, particularly if you can be very symmetrical with your workmanship. As this is an advanced project, I will not specify lengths of wires or gauges, which means you can make your necklace as large as you wish. You will have to try to make it by looking at the photos and following the general steps in this project. Use your own judgment in measuring filigree wire to make the necessary spirals and find the proportions for the different parts.

YOU WILL NEED
- filigree wire
- 18-gauge square wire
- **18-20** 2–6mm silver balls
- **15** freshwater pearls and head pins for making dangles
- round prong setting and faceted stone (under 5mm)
- **12** 4mm jump rings
- 16-18 in. (41-46cm) sterling chain with loops large enough to put jump rings through
- clasp of your choice

Time for Something a Little Bit "Fan"-cy

Although this project looks complicated, if you take it step by step, you'll find it's a lot simpler than it appears. You'll start with the center section, the fan, and then make the dangle at the bottom. The final components, the chain accents, are nothing more than Norwegian *kronesølv* earring components with a ball soldered in the middle of each one. (Refer back to Project 1, p. 46, if you need a refresher on making those parts.)

Make the Fan

1–7 Begin with a length of 18-gauge square wire long enough to make the V-shaped base of the fan **[1]**. As in Project 6 (p. 66), find the middle of this piece and notch it with a file **[2]**. Bend the wire at this notch, making a large V shape. Give the legs of the V a slight outward curve **[3]**.

Cut an additional 18-gauge square wire for the upper part of the fan, making it slightly longer than the distance between the two end points of the V. Again, give it a gentle curve **[4]**. File the ends of the V to fit snugly against the top wire **[5]**. Flux the joints and place solder chips, and then solder, pickle, and rinse **[6]**. Clip off the excess wire and file the corners to finish off the fan shape **[7]**.

8–22 Now, cut a length of filigree wire that will be long enough

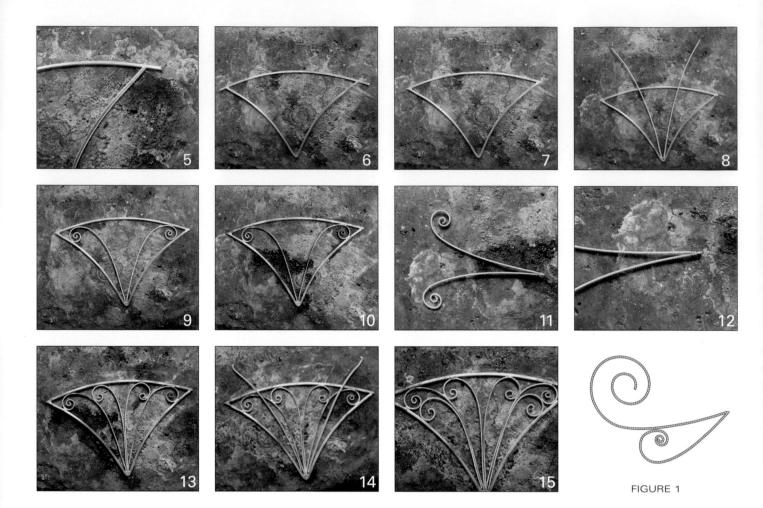

FIGURE 1

to make the two outermost spirals. You have to have enough wire to reach from the lowest point of the fan up beyond the top of the fan **[8]**, because you will need this excess to curl up into spirals. Remove the wire and curl the ends, basically creating a large witch's hat. Don't crimp the filigree wire in the middle, as you will need to place another witch's hat inside this one. Brace the witch's hat inside the framework and test for fit; the tension should hold the spirals nicely in each corner of the fan **[9]**. Add flux, place solder on all contact points, and solder, pickle, and rinse **[10]**.

Note: Long lengths of filigree wires in open designs melt more quickly than the wires in smaller, denser designs. Therefore, you will

have to watch this first piece to prevent melting it. The more wires you add to the piece, however, the less you have to worry about melting.

Next, make the middle two spirals the same way. This time, crimp the point of the witch's hat **[11]** and taper it with the base of your pliers. Increase the pressure as you get closer to the peak of the hat, which will create a sharp point **[12]**.

Fit the large witch's hat into the middle of the fan. Adjust the spirals in or out as necessary. Remember that symmetry is a must in this project. Keep the matching spirals at the same level in the fan. Flux, solder, pickle, and rinse **[13]**.

Now add the second row of spirals; one pair fits under the outer spirals, the other pair fits under the middle

spirals. You will have to make each wire separately as a single spiral, instead of making a witch's hat. Try to estimate the length you will need, including what you will need to make the spiral part. Cut each pair of wires at the same time to ensure the lengths are the same, and check the lengths by test-fitting the wire before making the spirals **[14]**.

Make matching spirals and work them into the framework inside the two outermost spirals. Keep them symmetrical. Flux, solder, pickle, and rinse **[15]**.

The long part of the inner spiral should be flush against the outer one. Make sure you place solder along this long joint and use your torch to drag melted solder along this joint; **[16]** shows a length of wire that needs to be

corrected, and **[17]** shows the correction after the addition of more solder.

Repeat step 14 to make the spirals that fit under the middle spirals. If you wish, you can make spirals, put them in place, cut off the excess wire, and again fit them **[18–20]**. Solder these new spirals in place, making sure you draw the solder up the length of the spirals **[21]**. This will add strength to the overall piece.

Once you've finished these central spirals, it's time to add some smaller filigree **[22]**.

• Make a large teardrop and place it between the center spirals, just under the center top of the framework.

• Make a matching pair of double spirals **[figure 1]**. Add a double spiral to each side of the fan at the top.

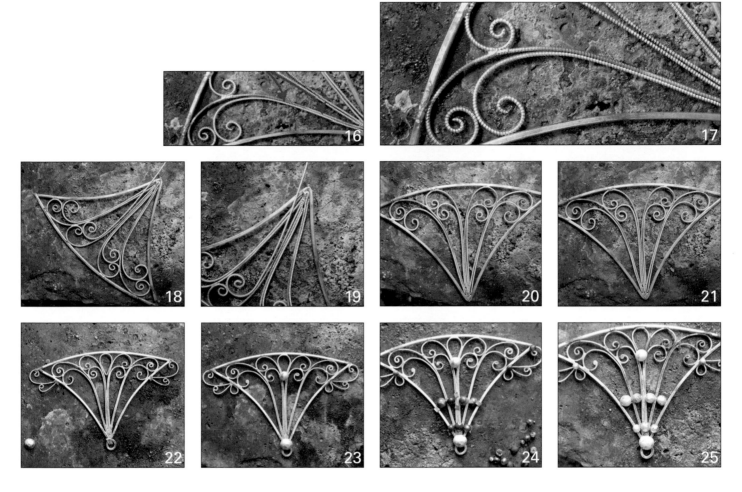

• File the bottom tip of the fan flat. Take a jump ring and close it tightly. File flat the top of the jump ring (at the opening). Place the flat side of the jump ring against the flattened tip of the fan; solder should close the jump ring and also attach it to the tip of the fan.

Flux, solder, pickle, and rinse the teardrop, double spirals, and jump ring. Break it down into more than one step if you need to.

23–27 Next, take two large balls and place one over the set of joints at the bottom of the fan and the other over the joint where the teardrop fits into the center of the spirals near the top of the fan. Also make two small filigree teardrops and add them below the double

spirals on the outside of the fan. Solder as usual [23].

Next, add several more silver balls. Starting at the bottom, place three small balls low on the fan, slightly above the large ball you just placed. (If you like, the center ball here can be slightly larger than the other two, which is what I did with this project.) Then, almost halfway up, place four medium balls between the wires of the internal spirals. Make them follow the curve of the top of the fan. Place four small balls over the joints where the outer filigree meets the framework, two on each side [24]. Solder, pickle, and rinse [25].

Finally, take two more jump rings, close them tight, and file the edge at the opening flat. Place them against the framework right

above the points where the outermost spirals are soldered to the top. Solder the jump rings in place. Add two matching balls straddling the jump ring and the framework [26]. The chain connects to the fan via these jump rings; the added strength created by the balls will ensure your piece doesn't fall apart under its own weight. When you have finished soldering the fan, it should look something like the one shown in photo [27]. If you look carefully, one of the spiral centers to the left is melted. If you have an accident like this in a symmetrical design, you can do a controlled melt of the corresponding spiral on the other side of the design. Make your mistakes look planned and no one will know the difference.

Make the Dangle and Accents

28–31 Now, on to the second part of the necklace: the filigree dangle below the fan. This part is pretty straightforward compared to the fan portion.

Begin by making a large teardrop framework out of 18-gauge square wire, as you did in Project 8 (p. 74). Use the same square wire to make a smaller teardrop to serve as the bail. Solder the framework and bail together, pickle, and rinse [28].

Next, make an elongated heart shape out of filigree wire, and place it point up into the framework. Solder the heart in place and solder the two spirals of the heart together. Add a silver ball over the joint where the heart, the small teardrop

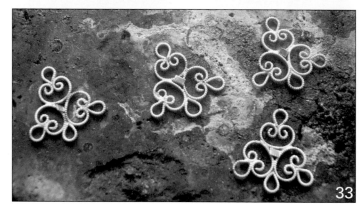

bail, and the large teardrop framework come together for strength [**29**]. Now add two teardrops, one large and one small, to the inside of the framework.

At the bottom of the piece in [**30**], add a modified lima bean shape. I use this shape quite a lot at the bottoms of pendants where I want to add a dangle. (In this case, it's a dangle on a dangle!) This shape is very simple: Just make a lima bean and bend the spirals backward, leaving a loop at the bottom [**figure 2**].

Solder a ball at the bottom center of the frame as well as where the small teardrop meets the two spirals. Finally, solder a small, round prong setting into the largest teardrop [**31**].

32–33
Make four of the trefoil earring dangles from Project 1, p. 46 [**32**]. Once you have completed the trefoils, solder four matching balls to the middle of the trefoils [**33**].

Finishing

34
Once you have the fan, dangle, and accents made, you need to burnish and polish all parts. Set the small faceted stone

FIGURE 2

FIGURE 3

in the prong setting when polishing is complete **[34]**.

Assembly

Now it's time to assemble the whole necklace (refer to the illustration above and the photo on p. 88). The general steps are as follows:

• Join the fan and the dangle with a jump ring.

• Divide your length of chain in two. Thread a sturdy jump ring that will fit through the cable in the chain through one end of each chain segment. Thread the jump rings onto each of the loops at the top of the fan.

• Make pearl drops as you did in Project 1. I suggest using three large freshwater pearls on the fan and dangle, and smaller pearls on the trefoils.

• After you have added the pearl drops to the accents, find four jump rings that fit through the chain and space the accents 1½ in. (3.8cm) out and 3 in. (7.6cm) out from the connection to the fan.

• Add a jump ring and the clasp of your choice to the back of the chain. Shorten the chain if necessary.

Variations

If you wish, use beads (instead of pearls) to match the accent stone you set on the dangle. You can also use shorter segments of chain and make bead accents between the segments, with or without the Norwegian trefoil accents. You can even make a series of trefoils or units with four limas and loops and link them as one continuous chain or as in-line accents in the chain. **Figure 3** shows two examples of good "clover" shapes that work as continuous chains.

Wings

Pearl dangles, a central faceted gemstone, and large silver balls highlight this winged design.

"Wings" is a design I've been doing since college. It's based on a flight theme, with a central stone, an open framework, and a lot of filigree spreading out like wings from a central point. I use the design mostly for necklaces, but some people who see it comment that the design would make a nice tiara if turned up rather than down as it is for a necklace (and they're right; I like to use this design for tiaras as well).

YOU WILL NEED
- 18-gauge square wire
- 16-gauge square wire
- filigree wire
- oval gemstone and setting
- 9 2–5mm silver balls
- 5 pearl dangles
- 4 4–5mm jump rings
- clasp of your choice

This is an advanced project. I will give you the pattern and show you how it is put together, but it's up to you to decide on lengths of wires. This means that you can decide how large or small the final piece should be. Just keep the proportion between filigree to gemstone a graceful one, and you'll do fine.

Let Your Creativity Take Flight . . .
Hopefully, at this point in the book, you've begun to get a feel for filigree and how it works. I find it to be a very intuitive and visual technique that allows you a degree of design freedom that many other jewelry-making disciplines do not. For instance, each piece you make can be different from the last. Designs can vary depending on stone shape and size. If something doesn't work out exactly as you have planned, you can change the design on the spot without destroying the overall feel of the piece. As you work on this last project and move on to your own designs, let your creativity take flight as though it, too, has wings.

One thing that makes this piece differ from the other projects is that you will use 16-gauge square wire for the main curving frame at the top of the piece, rather than the 18-gauge you've used for other frameworks. (Remember that the smaller the number in gauges, the thicker the wire; thus, 16-gauge square wire is thicker and stronger than 18-gauge square wire.) This is a large piece, and it requires extra support from its framework.

1 To begin, cut a strip of 16-gauge square wire to make the curved frame at the top. Cut a strip of 18-gauge square wire and begin by making a large lima bean shape, but then bend it backward from the middle. Position the frame and the lima together at their midpoints. Flux, solder, pickle, and rinse **[1]**.

2–3 Next, add the first three units of filigree. Make two double spirals (as you did for the outside of the fan in Project 11, p. 88). These spirals need to be large enough to reach from the 18-gauge frame to the end of the 16-gauge frame. The three spirals on each side (created by the double spiral you just added and one spiral from the 18-gauge framework) should make a fairly even diagonal line along the lower edge of each side of the necklace **[2]**.

Make a rounded lima shape to serve as the center piece. The setting will be placed in the center of this shape, so be sure to test-fit the setting to make sure the lima is large enough. Place solder chips on all contact points except the two spirals of the lima **[2]**. (This point should remain open until after you have soldered the setting in place, should you need to adjust the spirals to fit around it.) Solder, pickle, and rinse **[3]**.

4–5 Now we'll add the setting. I used an 18 × 14mm amethyst with a sterling-silver basket setting, but you can use any stone you like, and any setting (whether a prong setting or cabochon setting). Make sure the stone is large enough to balance all the filigree.

First, attach the setting where the round lima meets the 18-gauge frame **[4]**. Use any of these three methods (or any combination of the three). Pickle and rinse when finished.

• Place solder chips next to the prongs on the framework.

• Melt solder in place first, then remelt it to attach the setting.

• Use a solder pick to place the solder.

Lift the necklace and gently bend the curls of the large lima shape in toward the setting. They need to sit tightly up against the bottom of the setting and be centered **[5]**. Solder your contact points, including the point where the two spirals meet.

6–7 Once the setting is securely soldered in place, the basic framework for the rest of your pieces to fit into or onto is complete. Use the tension in the new filigree pieces to hold them in place within the existing filigree. Set up as many at one time as you can before you move to soldering. It will save you time. A piece like this usually takes three to four hours to craft, solder, and polish, so take any shortcuts you can.

Make two large spirals, similar to the 18-gauge framework **[6]**. Curve the tails of the spirals to fit flush against the lima shape in the center. Crimp/taper the end to fit as far up into the gap between the lima and the heavier frame as possible. If you can make the spirals meet the heavier

frame spirals and still look symmetrical, then go ahead and solder both at the tail of the spiral and the spiral itself. If not, solder the tails into the gap first, then pickle and rinse. Adjust the spirals after you have pickled and rinsed the piece, and then solder them in place.

Make three overlapped teardrops: two small and one large. Place and add solder chips [7]; note that the photo also shows adding chips to attach the two previous spirals to the 18-gauge frame. Solder as usual.

8–11 Make two teardrops, two double spirals, and one single spiral, and place them as indicated in [8]. Make your shapes approximately the size you need and adjust the spirals to make them fit

tightly into place. The tension of the unsoldered filigree units should make them stay put long enough for you to add the other pieces [9]. Add flux, place solder chips as indicated in [10], and solder the piece [11]. Solder the loose teardrops last, as they have nothing to hold them in place. Remember to warm the whole piece thoroughly before focusing the flame on the areas you want to solder.

Sometimes, you may need to turn the piece and use the torch from a different direction to get some of the solder to flow. Don't worry if you have to go over the piece more than once to get all the joints soldered correctly. Remember to pickle and rinse between attempts.

12–15 Add silver balls over the joints, using the illustration above as a guide. Use large balls for bigger joints and small balls on bare filigree [12–14]. Solder, pickle, and rinse. Make sure that the balls are secure.

Finally, cut off any excess wire at the ends of the 16-gauge framework and file them flat along a diagonal. Take two jump rings and make sure they are tightly closed. File each jump ring flat at the opening. Place the flat side of the jump rings against the flat ends of the framework [15]. Flux, solder, pickle, and rinse. Then solder a matching set of larger balls over the joint to add strength.

16 Once you have finished soldering, burnish and polish the piece. Set the stone and do any touch-up finishing around the setting [16].

Add five pearl drops to the five teardrop shapes along the bottom of the piece. Then, add a length of chain to each jump ring. (My piece has a chain of about 16 in./41cm in length, but feel free to choose the length you prefer.) It is best worn high on the neckline. Add a clasp half to each end of chain.

Congratulations! You've finished the final project.

gallery

Filigree spirals and teardrops combine with lapis and blue topaz in this pendant.

An asymmetrical piece can still have balance, as demonstrated by this tigereye and lemon quartz (citrine) necklace with beaded chain accents.

Although I enjoy using my lupin design (see Project 9) for asymmetrical stones, it works just as well with symmetrical stones. This pendant features dichroic glass highlighted by a cultured pearl.

Another Norwegian stone, larvikite, is sometimes marketed as "Norwegian moonstone." I've used it here with a cubic zirconia.

This piece, another variation on my lupin design, features thulite, Norway's national stone, as its focal point.

Combine three or more stones for a distinctive look. This piece features a North Carolina emerald tourmaline matrix with an emerald accent and a tourmalinated quartz dangle.

Be unconventional—you don't have to stick with traditional cabochons of faceted stones! This drusy is a piece of Tampa Bay agatized coral with a citrine accent.

Use nature as a guide. I often find my pieces develop into recognizable patterns. This piece, with a peridot setting, is reminiscent of an iris.

This filigree fan is set with a blue topaz, and features a pieced dangle composed of Afghan lapis and Australian opal.

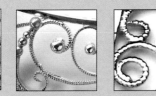

conclusion

LAST THOUGHTS ON DESIGN

mystic topaz
turquoise

I am quite sure that, as you worked on some of the projects, you thought about changing a spiral here or there, or thought of an entirely new design. That's why this chapter on designs is here, at the end of the book, rather than at the beginning. Now that you have actually experienced making filigree, you can better understand the process of creating a design.

So where do you go from here? You can continue to make the projects in this book, of course, but the ultimate goal is to begin making variations on these designs and, before long, your very own designs. I can teach you the technique and give you tips, tricks, and rough design rules, but in the end, it's up to you to take filigree and run with it, developing a unique style for yourself.

If no designs are leaping into your head, take a moment to turn back to the chapter on filigree (p. 7). Now, with a more experienced eye, look again at some of the diverse styles and techniques shown there. You may find your fingers itching to try re-creating some of those pieces!

To Each Their Own . . .

Different ways of designing work better for different people. For example, 90 percent of what I create is designed on the bench as I go. I begin with stones that I feel work together, figure out how I want them to sit in relation to each other, and then build the piece intuitively around them. I've worked with these materials and techniques for many years, so this approach works for me, but it won't for everyone. Many people need to plan out their designs in advance, sometimes making several designs before they find one that works. The following are a few suggestions on how you can approach making your designs in advance.

Drawing

Hand-drawing is an honored and ages-old means of designing. With filigree work, it's as easy as doodling little spirals, so sit down and draw. You can start by tracing your stones (if you're using any) onto paper and experimenting with different designs. You can even scan or photocopy the stones and print out several pages with just the stones in the desired proximity to each other, and then make different pencil drawings connecting them.

I draw designs from time to time, especially when I haven't had time to go to the studio and make pieces physically. For me, 80 percent of the fun is in the creative design process and not the actual construction. Thus, most of these designs,

This scan is from one of my doodle sessions. I haven't made any of these pieces yet, but the drawings give me ideas about what will work and what won't.

no matter how good or bad, never get off the paper!

Help! I Can't Draw!

So, what do you do if you can't draw? Some people are more hands-on creators. One suggestion I have is to physically build the piece first without soldering it. This means laying out the stones, cutting and shaping your units, and positioning the pieces until you've achieved the right arrangement.

The problem with this technique is that you end up with a bunch of small pieces that are hard to keep track of unless you somehow make a record of the pattern you've created. If you bump the table or if your cat jumps up, the pieces are likely to go flying, and you will have to start over! Another option is to take a digital picture of your design, print it out, and place the pieces with the image in a bag until you have a chance to solder them. This will work, but if you have a lot of similar but not identical parts, you could end up having a hard time getting the design the way you wanted it, even with the help of an image.

What I have done for years is this: Take a piece of cardboard a little larger than the piece you are going to make. The ideal cardboard is the thin cardboard from cereal boxes, frozen pizzas, and so on. Cut out the center of the cardboard so that you end up with a frame large enough to fit around the piece you are designing. Take wide (preferably clear) packing tape and stretch it across the opening of the frame. Flip the frame over, so the sticky side of the tape faces up. You'll end up with a work area that is sticky enough to hold your pieces in place while you design. You can pick them up and move them around, trying different arrangements until you are satisfied. When you are finished, take a piece of kitchen plastic wrap and press it over the piece you've designed and the exposed areas of the tape. As long as you treat it with reason-able care, this will hold your design until you are ready to solder it.

Make Your Mouse Work for You

For those of you who enjoy working on the computer, consider making a graphic file or template with the different filigree elements you might need. Add a file of scanned-in gemstones, either generic or specific to a given design, and do your layout on your computer. Each project in this book includes a computer-drawn diagram of what the finished piece should look like. Those drawings were made in this fashion.

PREPARING A DRAWN DESIGN

You can use this cardboard frame technique to prepare a drawn design, which is what I did with Project 12 (p. 94). One morning, I had to go to the mechanic's shop to get a small repair done on my car. I had time to kill, and I had sensibly brought along one of these tape-and-cardboard "easels," along with my drawing. I began to cut and lay out the pieces I needed for Project 12, using the drawing as a reference **[A–C]** and positioning the pieces on the tape while I sat at the repair shop. You basically build up your project just as you would do at the bench, but you have the option to go back and make changes before actually soldering.

When you are ready to make the piece, carefully pull or cut away the plastic wrap from the design. Use tweezers to remove the parts you wish to solder first, leaving the rest on the tape **[D]**. Transfer what you need section by section without having to hunt for loose pieces in a pile.

I taught this technique to my 12-year-old daughter. I made her a heart-shaped frame and then gave her a stone and some odds-and-ends spirals. From this, she used the cardboard framework and made her own design **[E]**.

I used a template like this to create the computer-drawn diagrams that accompany each project in this book.

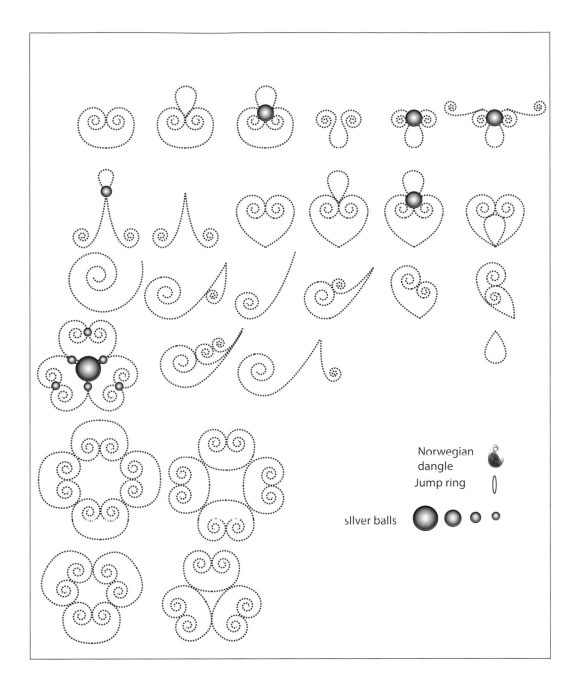

Norwegian dangle
Jump ring
silver balls

First, define how you want the lines to look. With filigree, a simple solution is to use a tightly dashed line 0.5mm thick. In some programs, you can define a style that can be applied over and over again and therefore be kept consistent. You can make a template based on this style, where basic units like the ones above are constructed. You can then copy and paste and scale these to make different designs.

There are many graphics programs out there, each with their own drawing interfaces. These were done in Adobe Illustrator CS, but similar patterns can be created in Freehand, Corel Draw, or other drawing programs. One tip: When scanning in your gemstones, remove the background and save in a format that allows transparency, such as Photoshop's .psd or .gif. That way, when you import the scans into your drawing program, the area around the stone will be transparent rather than opaque white. If the back-

ground is white, then it will cover surrounding filigree units unless placed in the backmost layer.

Once you have your templates, you can copy, paste, group, ungroup, and transform the units to make your theoretical designs. You can change stones, make variations on a theme, and print them out to scale. If you use a 100-percent scale, you can even tape the printout behind the cardboard frame so it is visible through the tape. Then use it as a guide.

Experiment

Try out the different design techniques and see what works for you. People are different, and what works for one does not work for all. Some people are theoretical designers and others are hands-on. Some are intuitive while others work better with logical, planned approaches.

Whichever approach you choose, here are a few things to remember when designing and making filigree jewelry.

Keeping a file of scanned-in gemstones allows easy designing of pieces like these.

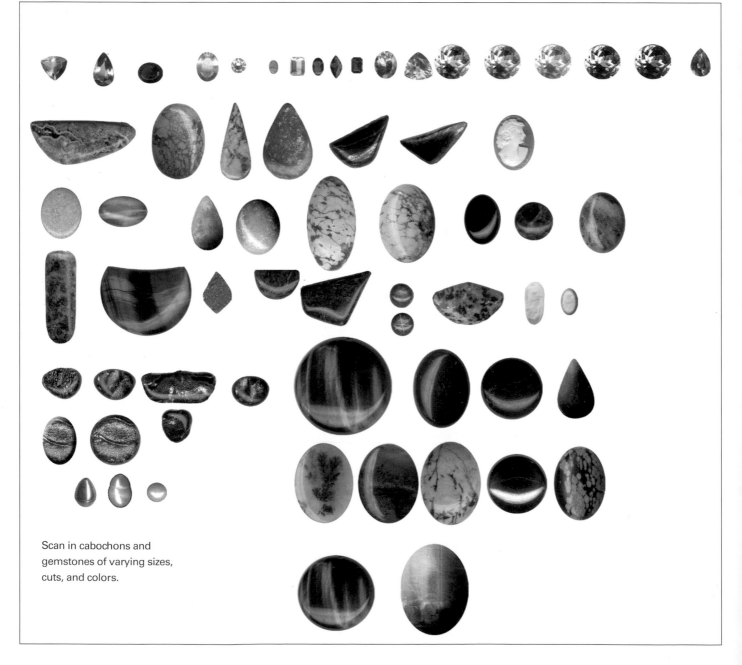

Scan in cabochons and gemstones of varying sizes, cuts, and colors.

Maintain structural integrity. This is perhaps the most important thing you need to learn when you experiment with new designs. What can you do to make the piece structurally sound?

• Use a framework of some kind to make your pieces more solid. In this book, I used 18- or 16-gauge square wire somewhere in the piece as a framework or anchor point for the filigree (with the exception of the first projects, which were very lightweight).

• Use silver balls to reinforce potential weak spots—especially connections, which bear the weight of the piece.

• Do not make pieces with too much air under a given spiral. Large spirals must have support from additional spirals, whether inside or next to them. If they don't, they will eventually bend out of shape.

• Make sure that you have enough contact points between filigree and heavy cabs to support the weight of the stone. Be aware of stress points and potential weak points.

Don't leave loose ends! I don't know how many times I've seen wireworkers leave loose ends on designs that could easily snag in hair or on sweaters. Be aware of open spirals and make sure they are soldered securely into place.

Balance is everything! In symmetrical designs, you have to be as precise as possible with making both sides of the design the same. Even asymmetrical designs, like Project 9 (p. 78) have to have a balanced feel and be balanced in the way they hang.

Remember your snail shells. Your design should include neat spirals with well-finished centers. The curves should seem natural in design. Use the inherent spring in the wire and your fingers to shape the pieces—don't force them by relying on pliers to shape pieces.

Don't get hung up on getting a piece perfect the first time around. Filigree is an art, and making filigree jewelry takes practice. The skills are not that difficult, but it does take time to get used to the feel of the wire, how it should fall into place as a whole, and how to solder it without melting it. Be patient with yourself, do your best, and move on to new pieces without discouragement.

Good Luck— and Enjoy

I hope you enjoyed this book and the projects in it. What's more, I'm hoping that you feel inspired to go on and create, and to help bring this art to North America. I would love to hear from you and hear your thoughts on filigree. If you design pieces you would like to share with other readers, please email me at bookdesigns@ jeannius.com. I will make a gallery with what comes in so that other readers may be inspired by your work as well as mine.

Enjoy, and best wishes to all my readers!

Manufacturers/Suppliers

Find jewelry-making and metalworking tools and supplies at the manufacturers and suppliers listed below. You can also attend local and national gem and mineral shows, and search eBay (ebay.com) for supplies.

Contenti
contenti.com
800-343-3364
Jewelry-making and metalworking tools and supplies

EuroTool
eurotool.com
800-552-3131
High-quality hand tools for jewelry-making

Fire Mountain Gems
firemountaingems.com
800-355-2137
Findings, settings, stones, and beads

Gesswein
gesswein.com
800-243-4466
Tools, equipment, supplies, and findings

Harbor Freight Tools
harborfreight.com
843-676-2603
Inexpensive tools, including files, pliers/cutters, and rolling mills

Hauser & Miller
hauserandmiller.com
800-462-7447
Metal supplier and refiner

Hoover & Strong
hooverandstrong.com
800-759-9997
Metalworking supplies, findings, and settings

Metalliferous
metalliferous.com
888-944-0909
Metal sheet, wire, and other jewelry-making supplies

Tripp's, Inc.
www.tripps.com
800-545-7962
Easy Mount settings, gems, chains, and tools

Artists

Jeanne Rhodes-Moen
jeannius.com

Lisa Gallagher
designsbylisag.com

Helen Goga
wirejeweler.com/helen_bio

Linda Shores Caristo
southernhighlandguild.org/lindacaristo/

Other Resources

Tumble Finishing for Handmade Jewelry, 4th edition, Judy Hoch, ISBN 0-9728269-0-4; order at marstal.com

http://groups.yahoo.com/group/silverthreads
I've set up this Yahoo group for questions about and discussion of *Silver Threads*.

resources